ARE YOU REALLY SAVED!?

ARE YOU REALLY SAVED!?

Bill Jackson

TATE PUBLISHING
AND ENTERPRISES, LLC

Published by Tate Publishing & Enterprises, LLC
127 E. Trade Center Terrace | Mustang, Oklahoma 73064 USA
1.888.361.9473 | www.tatepublishing.com

Tate Publishing is committed to excellence in the publishing industry. The company reflects the philosophy established by the founders, based on Psalm 68:11,
"The Lord gave the word and great was the company of those who published it."

Cover design by Niño Carlo Suico
Interior design by Gram Telen

Published in the United States of America

ISBN: 978-1-63268-729-6
1. Religion / Christian Life / General
2. Religion / Biblical Studies / General
15.03.12

Introduction

The Fathers will—What is His true will for our future with Him? You will learn his will and reasons why it is to be as He declared, and in a simplistic explanation of His desire for our lives, temporal and eternal. You will also see many deceptions perpetrated upon man, by men for their own agenda. There are also places in this writing that seem repetitive even redundant, but for good reason as you will see.

It is the will of the heavenly Father that all men be saved and come unto the knowledge of the truth. The truth is in many cases harder to comprehend or believe than the lies we are taught by other men. It is my prayer that all who read this come to the truth and make a good decision to follow in spirit and truth, so they may live and have the eternal life our Savior sacrificed for us all.

If you are an heir of salvation this should interest you and even help you make good decisions concerning your walk of truth. This can also help teach new believers some regular practices to keep and learn to apply to their lives and understanding. May the creator Yahweh bless you and keep you in His good way and truth.

This book may seem offensive to some but those seeking the truth it will bless. I am not against Christians, Catholics or any other religious named groups, we all have a duty to the Most High. This writing will free the masses from false worship and lies. If you are complacent and happy with church you probably are not a seeker of truth, but a follower of man and not the Most High. His opinion is the only one that will count in that final day, called the Great Day of Judgment. The man way will not save anyone. Not all people that have been on this earth will live eternal but those who do the will of the Father in heaven.

One day I heard this in my spirit: In that day, when heaven and earth collide, there will be no mercy for the guilty.

All scriptural references are from the King James Version the names of the Heavenly father and the son have been changed to the original names. The Father in heaven is YHWH, Yahweh, Father Yah, and the Son is Yahushua and means YHWH is Salvation. The term used for (god, God), is Elohim, elohim, El. There are several ways to spell the saviors name Yahushua, Yehoshua, Yashua, Yeshua, but Yesha is not a name it means save. We look to the one whose name means YHWH is Salvation.

ARE YOU REALLY SAVED?

If So! There are some things you should know.

This is a book about the knowledge of truth as the scriptures show us. You might want to share this with others and study in small groups. As iron sharpens iron your spirit may become shaper and more equipped with truth. The real question here is what you really know and how much does it affect your ability to receive the true unwatered down version of scriptural knowledge. Which is knowledge and truth that has not been watered down for easy acceptance. Many people do not like to be accused of any wrongdoing. They become angry, and some of them even turn away. The real reason for this book is to inform and not destroy. We all have a duty to seek the truth and become the everlasting sons of the Most High Heavenly Father. This is what He put on my heart to share with all the world, like it or not, remember the truth will set you free. Many people around the world make void His word do to lack of belief and their ideas of who HE is, or in short they try to do His thinking for Him! He told us we are not going to be greater than our Master because we are the clay, He is the potter. We are made in His image in His likeness man was made.

Genesis 1: [26] And Elohim said, Let us make man in our image, after our likeness: and let them have dominion over the fish of the sea, and over the fowl of the air, and over the cattle, and over all the earth, and over every creeping thing that creepeth upon the earth. [27] So Elohim created man in his own image, in the image of Elohim created he him; male and female created he them. [28] And Elohim blessed them, and said unto them, Be fruitful, and multiply, and replenish the earth, and subdue it: and have dominion over the fish of the sea, and over the fowl of the air, and over every living thing that moveth upon the earth. (Gen 1:26-28)

Now the question is? Where was Eve? he said let us make man in our image. Adam was the only one made, every creature was made on earth, and then named by Adam it was not until he was seen to be lonely or in inadequate that Eve was created and she was taken from Adams rib.

Mal 2: [13] And this have ye done again, covering the altar of YHWH with tears, with weeping, and with crying out, insomuch that he regardeth not the offering any more, or receiveth it with good will at your hand [14] Yet ye say, Wherefore? Because YHWH hath been witness between thee and the wife of thy youth, against whom thou hast dealt treacherously: yet is she thy companion, and the wife of thy covenant. [15] And did not he make one? Yet had he the residue of the spirit. And wherefore one? That he might seek a holy seed. Therefore take heed to your spirit, and let none deal treacherously against the wife of his youth. [16] For YHWH, the Elohim of Israel, saith that he hateth putting away: for one covereth violence with his garment, saith YHWH of hosts: therefore take heed to your spirit that ye deal not treacherously. (Mal 2:13-16)

Ok enough of that I was just challenging you to think and seek His revelation of this truth for your own understanding. Remember to ask daily for truth of His word and all things pertaining to your own walk. Let's go to the first sin, the sin of Eve after she was deceived and after the Heavenly Father pronounced the curses over the serpent, Adam and Eve.

Genesis 3: [21] Unto Adam also and to his wife did El Elohim make coats of skins, and clothed them.

It is evident the Heavenly Father loved His creation, and wanted them to live on and not die. It is written when we sin the life must be given for the price of sin, and the life is in the blood. That is why He slaughtered an animal and clothed them in the skins. The life of the animal was the price, it was ransomed for their lives to continue on. Because Adam no longer had the authority given to him, because of sin, after that the Father also proclaimed the order of man and wife.

Genesis 3: [16] Unto the woman he said, I will greatly multiply thy sorrow and thy conception; in sorrow thou shalt bring forth children; and thy desire shall be to thy husband, and he shall rule over thee.

And according to the scriptures they may not even perish.

[13] For Adam was first formed, then Eve. [14] And Adam was not deceived, but the woman being deceived was in the transgression. [15] Notwithstanding she shall be saved in childbearing, if they continue in faith and charity and holiness with sobriety. (1Tim 2:13-15)

Now you can see the awesome mercies of the Heavenly Father HalleluYah! She shall be saved in child bearing. Isn't that awesome. Eve or woman is to bear children and continue in faith, charity, and holiness with sobriety. The Heavenly Father has said we must not eat the blood of any animal or drink it why? Because the life is in the blood, when it is spilled the blood cries out to HIM after that His precious life force goes back to him, because HE is (omnipresent) that means He is in every living thing that is. He makes sure the evil goes into death. Remember the serpent who was also satan then stole his way into the heavenly gift by deception. He had stolen Adams authority over the earth. YHWH gave the earth to Adam to rule over and subdue, but Eve was deceived then they were both put in sin, and death ruled over them. This is why we were in need of a Savior to free us from the fear of death. Satan does not give up the dead. I would also like to say the death of the animal was a shadow and type of Messiah for what was to come. We all must be careful to walk as best we can in this end times, remember the original apostles also said the end times were then in that age. We know now they were a bit off since that was around 2000 years or so ago. But we do know for a fact the Anti Messiah spirit was already working in the earth to destroy the work of the Messiah.

1Jn 2:[18] Little children, it is the last hour: and as ye have heard that anti messiah shall come, even now are there many anti messiah; whereby we know that it is the last time.[19] They went out from us, but they were not of us; for if they had been of us, they would no doubt have continued with us: but they went out, that they might be made manifest that they were not all of us.[20] But ye have an unction from the Holy One, and ye know all things. [21] I have not written unto you because ye know not the truth, but because ye know it, and that no lie is of the truth. [22] Who is a liar but he that denies that Yahushua is the Messiah? He is anti Messiah that denies the Father and the Son. (1John 2:18-22)

That word anti has a meaning of (other or false, another) Strong's concordance G473 anti–an-tee' A primary particle; opposite, that is, (instead or because of) (rarely in addition to):–for, in the room of. Often used in composition to denote contrast, requital, (substitution), correspondence, etc.

And so for almost two thousand years there has been wars in the spirit of mans soul that has caused much confusion for our four fathers. We have more knowledge and scriptures available to us than they ever had even fifty years ago, this means we are without excuse.

3 For this is good and acceptable in the sight of Elohim our Saviour; [4] Who will have all men to be saved, and to come unto the knowledge of the truth. (1Tim 2:3-4)

Think about this wisely. What is all this for? Why is the Heavenly Father doing this work in us His creation? Remember that YHWH said, "Replenish the earth" in Genesis 1, which implies it may have been inhabited before us in this time. Let us not think He will not start over again, just when we think we know it all we find out He really is in charge. Regardless of what our so-called spiritual leaders say, His thoughts are much higher than ours. Man's righteousness is but filthy rags to HIM. Just something to remember! Also remember he had the Hebrews cast into captivity because of their evil ways, idolatries, and child sacrifices to false gods. It is as though He was regretful of His blessings upon them—even though it was the Torah that did them in because they stepped out from under His covering and sinned against Him. So they were under the curse and not blessings. You cannot walk in both. There is no middle ground—only a time of grace to allow repentance. But for some things, He does not allow a time of grace. Murdering His children is one such thing; because of that His wrath was kindled fiercely against them. I will share this with you about the reason for man's walking with Elohim; it is obvious to some. YHWH is restoring the heavens with His people a people who love Him and want to be with Him, no one in heaven will say they were forced to be there. And evil will be completely abolished, because we who are His and obedient to His will are the heirs of salvation. We are the replacement of satan and the angels that have been cast down to the darkness, which, was what the earth was before YHWH the Father restored it. Many think they are alright with the Father but do not know He will not let sin in His presence and will have nothing to do with sinners of any kind. So remember sin is sin no matter how great or small, it is the same to him. YHWH is looking for the Son of righteousness in us a complete inner man and mature Sons.

And I say unto you, That many shall come from the east and west, and shall sit down with Abraham, and Isaac, and Jacob, in the kingdom of heaven. 12 But the children of the kingdom shall be cast out into outer darkness: there shall be weeping and gnashing of teeth. (Mt 8:11-12)

Now who are the children? Those who never became reborn or those who became born again and even baptized into Yahushua but did not continue and mature they stayed children, those whom stayed drinking milk and not the meat of the word. And notice Yahushua was talking of great faith before that as He was saying even great faith was not enough, we must learn His ways and His word, His word is His will. So it is a truth we all must become knowledgeable in His ways and Torah. The word is what perfects us to become what He has called us to be and learn what He wants us to do. Now salvation is in His word and is of the Hebrews. (Both of the above are the children)

13 Yahushua answered and said unto her, Whosoever
drinketh of this water shall thirst again: 14 But whosoever
drinketh of the water that I shall give him shall never thirst;
but the water that I shall give him shall be in him a well of
water springing up into everlasting life. 15 The woman saith
unto him, Sir, give me this water, that I thirst not, neither
come hither to draw. 16 Yahushua saith unto her, Go, call
thy husband, and come hither. 17 The woman answered
and said, I have no husband. Yahushua said unto her, Thou
hast well said, I have no husband: 18 For thou hast had five
husbands; and he whom thou now hast is not thy husband:
in that saidst thou truly. 19 The woman saith unto him, Sir, I
perceive that thou art a prophet. 20 Our fathers worshipped
in this mountain; and ye say, that in Jerusalem is the place
where men ought to worship. 21 Yahushua saith unto her,
Woman, believe me, the hour cometh, when ye shall neither
in this mountain, nor yet at Jerusalem, worship the Father.
22 Ye worship ye know not what: we know what we worship:
for salvation is of the Jews. (John 4:13-22)

This is very important to see and know, I wonder did anything click in your mind just then? Yahushua was talking to a Samaritan woman at the well of Jacob. And she was given the revelation of who He was, as He said I am He, when she said the Messiah was going to tell us all.

YHWH was saving man all along each time He gave more and more of Himself for mans completion and restoration of the inner being. That is His desire for us to become as the angels of YHWH. Because we are to replace those cast down from the heavenly place. Everything we go through is a trial, that which does not stop us or make us give up, improves us and makes us better. We must look at the function of sin or the darkness within, so let's look at first mention of it in the scriptures.

6 And YHWH said unto Cain, Why art thou wroth?
and why is thy countenance fallen?

7 If thou doest well, shalt thou not be accepted? and if
thou doest not well, sin lieth at the door. And unto thee
shall be his desire, but you should rule over him. (Gen 4:6-7)

This is of the utmost importance to hear and adhere to, because this is a simple way to look at many problems. When ever you are doing wrong the door to death is open wide. But when you do good, and keep sin out of your heart, the door is shut and therefore cannot enter into your soul. We are to rule over sin and not give into temptations of the flesh or wrong doings. See how Cain was angry and jealous of his brother, the battle field is in the mind when you give into the evil thoughts, those thoughts become actions in the physical almost every time. Here is an example of not having a choice once sin opens the door.

25In meekness instructing those that oppose themselves;
if Elohim peradventure will give them repentance to the

acknowledging of the truth; [26] And that they may recover themselves out of the snare of the devil, who are taken captive by him at his will. (2Tim 2:25-26)

See the blessing of repentance is a clean heart and freedom from the curse. Sin is a curse to your soul, every time you are in sin the door is open to many evils and bad things. Sin is the reason many people are sick, and encounter hardships beyond their control. Those things carry over into the next generations as well; thus, they become generational curses! Many people blame the system or society for their hard ships and dysfunctional lives, I say to all who read this, many are under generational curses from their past generations. That is why we must confess the sins of our forefathers and break off those generational curses. Also confess our own to become completely free of them as well, now it will not be a big deal for some but for others it will mean life and turning to truth. Sin controls a persons actions and thoughts, the deeper into the darkness the more control sin has. I also will show you this truth of freedom from sin, the scriptures is the power of YHWH. When spoken by a person who owns the verse or the scripture, the authority and power of the word goes forth into the hearing of the sinning persons and pushes back the darkness to start life in the hearer. When the word convicts, condemns and causes the sinner to back up, that is the sin within turning the person away from the hearing of the word, sin does not want to be cast out. Also with each and every confession of wrong doing the sin leaves with the speaking and can no longer stay in because that is a part of ruling over it! There also are many things we do not know about that which causes spiritual death, for instance racism, it is death to the oppressed and the oppressor. Because un forgiveness is sin, it is a catalysts to the door of death. And the door can only be closed by true repentance and forgiveness, it is a wrong to YHWH. He is the one who must hear to open the eyes of the repented soul. I know, because I went through the process, many years ago. Racism is a sin because of hate most of the times it is generational, but let me say, I never was a racist at all even while growing up, but, there was always a barrier there that kept me from truly being at ease when I was around other races. I really had no idea there was a stumbling block there, but there was and it was a bad one. I was in my late 30s when I was learning the word and going through many trials a lot of them were generational curses and bad choices of marriage. But in my learning I was at a place where I was one of five caucasians in a group of hundreds. One day It was impressed on my spirit to apologize to an African American man for what my forefathers did to his forefathers. I heard it and did just that, the man I was speaking to did not receive what I said, another man with him realized what was happening and he did receive the apology as I asked for forgiveness, something inside my soul exploded and I was in tears weeping without control I was released from a generational curse. That is why we must confess our generational sins. Seek forgiveness for all your wrongs because it becomes a blessing to draw you closer to the creator YHWH. He forgives us when we come to Him and confess our wrongs! I never even hardly new any of my forefathers, to even know they had those problems. So I praise Yahweh the Father for His faithfulness, loving kindness and direction in my life HalleluYah! Praise Yahweh! So as you can see forgiveness is a catalyst toward a cleansed heart just as un forgiveness is a catalyst toward death. YHWH spoke that to Cain even when there was no laws of salvation at that time in mans history. Remember YHWH wants us to rule over sin, not the other way around. We have a much better way to walk with Yahushua in this covenant of life, because Yahushua has taken all upon Himself and given us freedom from sin. He conquered death and the grave, and came up with the keys to death and now we can become sons of YHWH. HalleluYah!

There have been many types of Messiah and forms of salvation since the beginning. The story of Cain and Able was a shadow type of yearly sacrifice done in the time of the tent of meeting. when the Ark of the covenant was with the Israelites. Cain was set free with a mark, like a scapegoat. And Ables blood spilled as if he were the sacrifice. Abraham and his son Yitshaq / Isaac Was a shadow type of YHWH sending His only Beloved Son Yahushua as the sacrifice, and YHWH spoke from the heavens, Abraham would possess the gates of his enemies and YHWH blessed him. There is also where Abraham called that place YHWH Yireh which is YHWH (sees) and because He sees, He provides. HalleluYah! In my opinion one of the most awesome to see is the tent of meeting the Ark of the Covenant, and the meanings of the different parts of it. Many do not know, that was a replica of the Messiah Yahushua and the Heavenly Father in the heart and soul of man. It was a replica of the living Tabernacle to come! Even circumcision was a shadow of the salvation of YHWH for His children. You see it was a covenant with Abraham and all his descendants before the covenant with Messiah Yahushua. When the child was born they counted off eight days then circumcised the new born sons. The doctors found out the coagulation time was about seven days, the 8th day represent the last great day! The day of reckoning, YHWH has the whole world on a time frame the first part has been mans time to multiply, grow in understanding, and become what YHWH has called us to be in our inner man. Then is the beginning of the 1000 year millennium. Then after that is when there will be judgment for all, although man is not sure when the clock truly started. Then those whom are of the covenant with Abraham before Messiah that keep His word and walked rightly will become circumcised of heart, there spiritual flesh heart will be circumcised by YHWH HalleluYah! And it even goes farther than that, Yahushua will purge them all that are YHWH's. You see all those that lived and walked with YHWH from the days of (Mosheh / Moses) are under the covenant of life through the working of YHWH in Moses they are all a work in the likeness of Moses and are not able to be completed until Messiah completes them, by His likeness. Hence forth He will Purge and cleanse them that are under the covenant made with Moses through the Father Yahweh.

2 But who may abide the day of his coming? and who
shall stand when he appeareth? for he is like a refiner's fire,
and like fullers' soap: 3 And he shall sit as a refiner and
purifier of silver: and he shall purify the sons of Levi, and
purge them as gold and silver, that they may offer unto
YHWH an offering in righteousness. 4 Then shall the
offering of Yudah and Yerusalem be pleasant unto YHWH,
as in the days of old, and as in former years. 5 And I will
come near to you to judgment; and I will be a swift witness
against the sorcerers, and against the adulterers, and against
false swearers, and against those that oppress the hireling in
his wages, the widow, and the fatherless, and that turn aside
the stranger from his right, and fear not me, saith YHWH
of hosts. 6 For I am YHWH, I change not; therefore ye sons
of Jacob are not consumed. (Mal 3:2-6) See (John 14:6).

Now you can see the Ark of the Covenant and the tent of meeting is all a shadow picture of Messiah Yahushua, the whole thing replicates us and Him in our hearts and souls. Because Messiah had not come yet they are in the Moses likeness, and incomplete. Now all who are under the covenant with YHWH before Mosheh are also going to be purged and cleansed by Yahushua Ha Meshiyach also, because they walked with YHWH and are His. Remember no one comes to the Father except through the Son! All those that are still keeping the covenant of Mosheh after the death burial resurrection of Messiah Yahushua some 2000 years ago are no longer able to be heirs in the Mosheh likeness. Now! Yahushua is the only way to have life eternal here is the proof!

Psalm and prayer of Dawid.

1 Hear the right, O YHWH, attend unto my cry, give
ear unto my prayer, that goeth not out of feigned lips. 2
Let my sentence come forth from thy presence; let thine
eyes behold the things that are equal. 3 Thou hast proved
mine heart; thou hast visited me in the night; thou hast
tried me, and shalt find nothing; I am purposed that my
mouth shall not transgress. 4 Concerning the works of men,
by the word of thy lips I have kept me from the paths of
the destroyer. 5 Hold up my goings in thy paths, that my
footsteps slip not. 6 I have called upon thee, for thou wilt
hear me, O YHWH: incline thine ear unto me, and hear
my speech. 7 Shew thy marvelous lovingkindness, O thou
that savest by thy right hand them which put their trust in
thee from those that rise up against them. 8 Keep me as the
apple of the eye, hide me under the shadow of thy wings, 9
From the wicked that oppress me, from my deadly enemies,
who compass me about. 10 They are enclosed in their own

fat: with their mouth they speak proudly. [11] They have now compassed us in our steps: they have set their eyes bowing down to the earth; [12] Like as a lion that is greedy of his prey, and as it were a young lion lurking in secret places. [13] Arise, O YHWH, disappoint him, cast him down: deliver my soul from the wicked, which is thy sword: [14] From men which are thy hand, O El Elohim, from men of the world, which have their portion in this life, and whose belly thou fills with thy hid treasure: they are full of children, and leave the rest of their substance to their babes. [15] As for me, I will behold thy face in righteousness: I shall be satisfied, when I awake, with thy likeness.

(Psalm 17:1-15)

Dawid a man after YHWH's own heart knew this truth, and he even had that knowledge of Yahushua as the Elohim of salvation. Yahushua means Yahweh is salvation!! Here is proof!

[1] YHWH said unto my Master, Sit thou at my right hand, until I make thine enemies thy footstool. [2] YHWH shall send the rod of thy strength out of Zion: rule thou in the midst of thine enemies. [3] Thy people shall be willing in the day of thy power, in the beauties of holiness from the womb of the morning: thou hast the dew of thy youth. [4] YHWH hath sworn, and will not repent, Thou art a priest for ever after the order of Melchizedek. [5] The Master at thy right hand shall strike through kings in the day of his wrath. [6] He shall judge among the heathen, he shall fill the

places with the dead bodies; he shall wound the heads over many countries. [7] He shall drink of the brook in the way: therefore shall he lift up the head. (Psalm 110:1-7)

You do remember Melchizedek He was also spoken of when Abraham came back after the war he won for the Sovereigns of Sodom and Amorah and brought Lot and all his possessions back. Melchizedek was the priest that blessed Abram [17] And the king of Sodom went out to meet him after his return from the slaughter of Chedorlaomer, and of the kings that were with him, at the valley of Shaveh, which is the king's dale. [18] And Melchizedek king of Salem brought forth bread and wine: and he was the priest of the Most High Elohim. [19] And he blessed him, and said, blessed be Abram of the most high El Elohe, possessor of heaven and earth: [20] And blessed be the Most High El Elohe, which hath delivered thine enemies into thy hand. And he gave him tithes of all. (Gen 14:17-20)

You see that was the King of kings Yahushua the one who liveth forever, and is the right hand of YHWH.

[1] For this Melchezedek, king of Salem, priest of the most high Elohim, who met Abraham returning from the slaughter of the kings, and blessed him; [2] To whom also Abraham gave a tenth part of all; first being by interpretation King of righteousness, and after that also King of Salem, which is, King of peace; [3] Without father, without mother, without descent, having neither beginning of days, nor end of life; but made like unto the Son of YHWH; abideth

a priest continually. [4] Now consider how great this man was, unto whom even the patriarch Abraham gave the tenth of the spoils. [5] And verily they that are of the sons of Levi, who receive the office of the priesthood, have a commandment to take tithes of the people according to the law, that is, of their brethren, though they come out of the loins of Abraham: [6] But he whose descent is not counted from them received tithes of Abraham, and blessed him that had the promises. [7] And without all contradiction the less is blessed of the better. [8] And here men that die receive tithes; but there he receiveth them, of whom it is witnessed that he liveth. [9] And as I may so say, Levi also, who receiveth tithes, paid tithes in Abraham. [10] For he was yet in the loins of his father, when Melchizedek met him. [11] If therefore perfection were by the Levitical priesthood,

(for under it the people received the Torah or law,) what further need was there that another priest should rise after the order of Melchizedek, and not be called after the order of Aaron? [12] For the priesthood being changed, there is made of necessity a change also of the law. [13] For he of whom these things are spoken pertained to another tribe, of which no man gave attendance at the altar. [14] For it is evident that our Master and Savior sprang out of Yehudah; of which tribe Moses spake nothing concerning priesthood.[15] And it is yet far more evident: for that after the similitude of Melchizedek there ariseth another priest, [16] Who is made, not after the law of a carnal commandment, but after the power of an endless life. 17 For he testifieth, Thou art a priest for ever after the order of Melchizedek. 18 For there is verily a disannulling of the commandment going before for the weakness and unprofitableness thereof. 19 For the law made nothing perfect, but the bringing in of a better hope did; by the which we draw nigh unto YHWH. 20 And inasmuch as not without an oath he was made priest: 21 (For those priests were made without an oath; but this with an oath by him that said unto him, YHWH sware and will not repent, Thou art a priest for ever after the order of Melchizedek:) 22 By so much was Yahushua Ha Mashiyach made a surety of a better testament. (Heb 7:1-22)

We who are in Messiah are already circumcised in heart through the work of Yahushua and the Father YHWH whom sealed us for the last great day and eternal life. The reason for that was time, man was not able to completely forgive with unconditional love and forgiveness. Only through Yahushua Ha Messiah in our souls are we able to accomplish true repentance with unconditional forgiveness and love. And that is a gift of Yah the Father to us all whom believe upon the Son Yahushua Ha Messiah. Those who reject the true Messiah Yahushua will not see life eternal, He is the one that will purge the sons of Lewi.

3 And he shall sit as a refiner and purifier of silver: and he shall purify the sons of Levi, and purge them as gold and silver, that they may offer unto YHWH an offering in righteousness. (Mal 3:3)

How awesome is that, what love and power, Thank you YHWH for your beloved Son Yahushua who will cleanse and purge your beloved chosen peculiar people HalleluYah!

The term Hebrew has a very important meaning "one from beyond".

1 And Abram went up out of Egypt, he, and his wife,
and all that he had, and Lot with him, into the south. 2
And Abram was very rich in cattle, in silver, and in gold. 3
And he went on his journeys from the south even to Bethel,
unto the place where his tent had been at the beginning,
between Bethel and Hai; 4 Unto the place of the altar, which
he had made there at the first: and there Abram called on
the name of YHWH. (Gen 13:1-4)

I want to show you an important fact of relationship and learning about YHWH, the scripture says Abram called upon the name of YHWH! HalleluYah aren't you glad he did. Because of that we all can become heirs of salvation in YHWH! Because if anyone be in Yahushua Ha Messiah he is the seed of Abraham and heir according to the promise. (Gal 3:29)

9 That if thou shalt confess with thy mouth the Master
Yahushua Ha Mashiyach, and shalt believe in thine
heart that YHWH hath raised him from the dead, thou
shalt be saved. 10 For with the heart man believeth unto
righteousness; and with the mouth confession is made unto
salvation. 11 For the scripture saith, Whosoever believeth on
him shall not be ashamed. (Rom 10:9-11)

It remains to be known by many a believer, we all must confess, same as to call upon the savior Yahushua Ha Mashiyach in order to have His spirit of true sight. See how Abraham called upon YHWH to sacrifice and please the creator in worship and for his words to be heard by YHWH. We must do the same!

[3] Yahushua answered and said unto him, Verily, verily, I say unto thee, except a man be born again, he cannot see the kingdom of YHWH. (John 3:3)

Many do not realize the true meaning of this scripture, Yahushua said you must be born again, not by flesh but of Spirit and by the only true Spirit of life, His own, and no other. We are all born in the likeness of Adam or Eve! So the spirit of sight and life does no longer dwell in the sons of man until the day of spiritual rebirth. One most important thing to see in our own walking is this. Whom you serve is your spiritual leader and is what your inner likeness resembles. If you have called upon and are baptized into Yahushua your inner man is in His likeness. So is same if you are serving familiar spirits you are in that likeness, but in all cases each one of us that are human has a spiritual inner likeness of some deity or what we may perceive as a deity. Each and every one of us born is in darkness as the word says, and we have no inner form because of the first sin. We are in the form of darkness, which is the likeness of satan.

In the beginning Elohim created the heaven and the earth. 1:2 and the earth was without form, and void; and darkness was upon the face of the deep. And the Spirit of Elohim moved upon the face of the waters. (Gen 1:1-2)

Now see the correlation, we are all from the earth and without inner form. Then when we call upon the creator YHWH he sends us to HIS Son, Yahushua the Messiah, He is the one who gives us the Spirit to see and receive the revelations of His word. We learn then and are brought into knowledge and empowerment of His scriptural revelations. Now all of us must become baptized into His likeness, which is a spoken law of salvation by Yahushua Ha Mashiyach.

28:18 And Yahushua came and spake unto them, saying, all power is given unto me in heaven and in earth. 28:19 Go ye therefore, and teach all nations, baptizing them in the name of the Father, and of the Son, and of the Holy Spirit: 28:20 Teaching them to observe all things whatsoever I have commanded you: and, lo, I am with you alway, even unto the end of the age. (Mt 28:18-20)

The true revelation is in the name of His Son Yahushua the Messiah. If anyone is in the world they are without inner form, unless they serve familiar spirits or demons that likeness will give them away in the end, none will be able to lie their way into heaven, they will look like mighty one remember YHWH said do not do to Him as the heathens or gentiles did to their gods. He was very clear on that subject because they sacrificed their children and many other things that lead to death. This is also spoken in the scriptures by Yahushua the Messiah concerning the plan of Salvation for all man kind.

Yahushua answered, Verily, verily, I say unto thee, except a man be born of water and of the Spirit, he cannot enter into the kingdom of YHWH. (John 3:5)

Being born of water, many also say born again by the water of the word. But in all reality they work together toward the completion of our inner being, to become like Yahushua. None can come to the Father Yah without the true likeness of Salvation sent by the Father for us all. As scriptures say none can come to the Father with out the Son! Many may argue what about the thief on the cross? Well he died before Yahushua was lifted up and put in the place of full authority, remember He said this day you will be with me in (Paradise) which also means future. Then many days later Yahushua had all authority in heaven and earth then spoke that we all must be baptized in the name of all authority. Now if you had not thought it to be necessary then reconsider your doctrinal belief, it is a must. You can realize YHWH has made it a very important thing to be known by the Son, so there is no mistake all who are there in the end, are there by choice and not force. He has made many fail safes to protect the true Kingdom of heaven by making sure none can enter in like a thief or a robber. It is easy to get completely lost in the spiritual realms when you are not in the true Spirit. There are many places of deception and false spirits that lure you away into an abyss you cannot find your way out of. How lost will a person be if following false spirits that deceive and cannot save. More have succumbed to the lies of false spirits than can be imagined. Just look at all the different doctrinal beliefs about salvation written down in other religions. How many denominations are actually in the Christian belief these days? It boggles the mind at what some people say salvation really is in today's society. It even boggles the mind even more when you see just how lightly many consider the plan of salvation and the true ways of the creator, it is a true sign of end times. Why many people would rather watch spiritual movies of evil entities than spiritual truth's, is because those spiritual things are witchcraft and sorcery. And like many gentile nations they all had served those things in times and generations past, it is the way they were. But those things lead to death, they sow dead thoughts into your souls and not life. This age is coming to the end of itself. Just think the depths of darkness in today's society and the evils that have become so common in this age compared to some years ago. These things boggle the mind and even cause many to fear and over react to normal every day situations. We know by the scriptures salvation is the work of the Father in us all who He draws to Himself. Although many believe! But they are not walking in His true way or His true Spirit of life.

Proverbs 8:17 I love them that love me; and those that seek me early shall find me.

It is also known everyone on this earth has a time to look and seek, in this day and age there is no excuse. So now we all have an open door to the Fathers favor through His beloved Son Yahushua Ha Mashiyach. By His gift of life and acknowledging YHWH's Yahushua and His working for eternal life. This brings us to the working of Yahushua in us, He who is our anointing our spirit of sight and life!

3 For we ourselves also were sometimes foolish, disobedient, deceived, serving divers lusts and pleasures, living in malice and envy, hateful, and hating one another. 4 But after that the kindness and love of Elohim our Saviour toward man appeared, 5 Not by works of righteousness which we have done, but according to his mercy he saved us, by the washing of regeneration, and renewing of the Holy Spirit; 6 Which he shed on us abundantly through Yahushua Ha Mashiyach our savior; 7 That being justified by his grace, we should be made heirs according to the hope of eternal life. 8 This is a faithful saying, and these things I will that thou affirm constantly, that they which have believed in YHWH might be careful to maintain good works. These things are good and profitable unto men. (Titus 3:3-8)

18 We know that whosoever is born of Elohim sinneth not; but he that is begotten of Elohim keepeth himself, and that wicked one toucheth him not. 19 And we know that we are of YHWH, and the whole world lieth in wickedness.

[20] And we know that the Son of YHWH is come, and hath given us an understanding, that we may know him that is true, and we are in him that is true, even in his Son Yahushua Ha Mashiyach. This is the true Elohim, and eternal life. (1John 5:18-20)

Again His express image is brought to us in the Spirit of Yahushua the beloved for our eternal life in Him. Remember it was the same Holy Spirit that entered into the womb of Miriam whom YHWH chose to bring Yahushua into this earth for us to be saved. That was called the washing and regeneration of the Holy Spirit. And only one other person was born with this Holy Spirit besides Yahushua that person was John the baptized or immerser, because He was chosen, for ordained by YHWH to fulfill a work in this earth, HalleluYah! And I am so glad He did!

Strong's meaning of (Regeneration)- G3824 paliggenesia -pal-ing-ghen-es-ee'-ah] n.f, From 3825; translates as "regeneration" 1 new birth, reproduction, renewal, recreation, regeneration.

G3825- palin–pal'-in] adv, from the same as 3823; (through the idea of oscillatory repetition) translates as "again" 142 times. 1 anew, again. 1A renewal or repetition of the action. 1B again, anew. 2 again, i.e. further, moreover. 3 in turn, on the other hand.

The word (new and renew) have a very important roll in the meaning of this word. This is a significant and most fundamental principal of YHWH's work in man, for He

(YHWH) so loved the world He gave His only begotten Son. His word says that the love of the world is enmity with the Father but His love is for the lost souls of mankind not the worldly lust of the flesh. This is why we must become born again, and that life is the spirit of favor with the heavenly Father YHWH. Why? Because the Torah is the perfect way to attain liberty from death. But as it is written man could not keep the law! Why? Because of perfect love. The law is only conquered through the perfect love of YHWH! HalleluYAH! Guess what? That perfect love was not in man until Yahushua Ha Mashiyach gave Himself for use to live eternal. Only His immense love could truly overcome all the hurts and pains in our soul caused by the worldly influences of life and existence. The love I'm talking about is love unconditional without boundries without limit that overcomes all the evils of the world.

33These things I have spoken unto you, that in me ye might have peace. In the world ye shall have tribulation: but be of good cheer; I have overcome the world. (John 16:33)

You can see what Yahushua meant, His love, His words, His ways, His work, His teaching us has overcome the world and all the evil lustful influences- influences that kill the soul of His creation. For YHWH so loves His people, He gave His only begotten Son, so all who would believe on Him should not perish but have everlasting life. See what Yahushua said about the law of love.

[4] Hear, O Israel Yahweh our Elohim is one: [5] And thou shalt love YHWH thy Elohim with all thine heart, and with all thy soul, and with all thy might. [6] And these words, which I command thee this day, shall be in thine heart: [7] And thou shalt teach them diligently unto thy children, and shalt talk of them when thou sittest in thine house, and when thou walkest by the way, and when thou liest down, and when thou risest up. [8] And thou shalt bind them for a sign upon thine hand, and they shall be as frontlets between thine eyes. [9] And thou shalt write them upon the posts of thy house, and on thy gates. (DE 6:4-9)

[37] Yahushua said unto him, Thou shalt love YHWH thy Elohim with all thy heart, and with all thy soul, and with all thy mind. [38] This is the first and great commandment. [39] And the second is like unto it, Thou shalt love thy neighbour as thyself. [40] On these two commandments hang all the law and the prophets. (Mat 22:37-40)

In the days before Yahushua took upon Himself all our sin man was unable to keep even these two commands. Only by the Spirit of life (Yahushua) in us are we able to truly forgive and love unconditionally! HalleluYah! The heavenly Father YHWH new man would have to be renewed in Spirit before this could happen. Remember Adam was filled with the spirit of life from the Father YHWH so he could live and be a eternal being on earth with YHWH and His Son Yahushua.

[14] Nevertheless death reigned from Adam to Moses, even over them that had not sinned after the similitude of Adam's transgression, who is the figure of him that was to come. (Rom 5:14)

Adam was he that was to come, we all were to have the Adam likeness, spiritually! He was a man in life but sin put him in death and so we all had the spirit of death upon our heads. Adam and Eve was the ones we were all fashioned after. So the washing and regeneration of the Holy Spirit was the beginning of the restoration of His people back into life. This means Jews, gentiles, and all men and woman, from all walks and creeds. Now the real truth is something you as an individual should ask for every day in prayer, which manner of teaching you adhere to such as denomination or who you follow be it Yahushua or another, you are responsible for you and your family. But I will warn each and every one who reads this there is only one way and man cannot make his own way into the heavenly place. Mans righteousness is but filthy rags to the Father of all creation. Every instance in the scriptures is a lesson for us all to learn from. And YHWH is always using His word to sharpen His people, thus the wonderful jewels of knowledge and wisdom that proceed out of His word. There are always patterns of life and death portrayed in His word, for us to learn from. All that was written in the scriptures is to teach us His desire, His ways for our futures, and His mannerisms so we can know Him by

His word. Just like a father teaches his children how to become good adults. YHWH's word is for us to become good mature spiritual beings – in short sons of YHWH. So let me show you a picture of repetition in man and the Fathers love over and over again. History seems to always repeat it self, and we like all the generations past always see our own future in the scriptures as we read and study them. Almost all of us can see the shadows of things to come. Adam and Eve are a shadow of all the marriages, because it is YHWH's design for man to be fruitful and replenish the earth. And so we see the evils of the world attack and try to destroy those righteous marriages, they are attacked because of there future in YHWH. But remember the first sin, YHWH's love over came His wrath, because from that day on all man was born into death. His love was for His future Son Yahushua to overcome, because Yahweh sees the beginning from the end. This means when He makes a decision to do something it always has an ending before He even does it. Now see what that means when YHWH slew the lamb and clothed Adam and Eve and showing them favor over death. YHWH proved to us all in that action His immense love for us! And His desire to save us from the curse of death even then. Nothing has changed in that manner He still has gone out of His way to save us all along even despite our wrong thinking and selfish ways. Our Father Yah was patient and long suffering as He waited for the creation to call upon the creator for the relationship, the fellowship of worship and love, and obedience to His way for our future with Him. The Father YHWH is omnipresent. He is the conscience that stops us from doing wrongs against our fellow man. But He still has given us free will to do as we must good or bad. Some cannot be obedient or stop being mean and evil, this is true of those whom have seared their conscience and can no longer here the voice of reason in themselves. Many persons on this earth take for granted the voice of conscience because they only hear it once in a while, and many say their heart leads them. But if so do remember the heart of man deceives [26] He that trusteth in his own heart is a fool: but whoso walketh wisely, he shall be delivered. (Proverbs 28:6)

All who are believers in the Scriptures and have the spirit of life in them are aware of the power of the Spirit in the Word because it is not just a book but the way to eternal life. So in order to understand it, one must have the true Spirit of Life—Yahushua Ha Mashiyach who is the teacher and life in us who believe. This is why the Scriptures tell us none come to the Father except by the Son. When the spirit-filled believer prays for the Father to save someone, He does just that, saves them from themselves and death. When we come to the Father, He sends us to His Son who brings us into the sight of His word. And the spirit of love to forgive and give us favor with the Father in Heaven. Because that is His word. Now there is another messiah spoken of in the Scriptures a false messiah. One that does as the original but keeps people from the real true way and life eternal. One that teaches to disregard the Scriptures and truth for man's ways and traditions. This is the other spoken of in the books of 1 John, Titus, 2 Peter, Jude, and so on. Throughout the epistles, the apostles warned all the flocks and ministers of the false teachers and those bringing in the teachings of another messiah, who perverts the true way and leads people away from the true Messiah, Yahushua. Now you can see YHWH has allowed this to bring in the true followers of Messiah, and only those really seeking the truth will find His the real way.

[21] Not everyone that saith unto me, Master, Master, shall enter into the kingdom of heaven; but he that doeth the will of my Father which is in heaven. [22] Many will say to me in that day, Master, Master, have we not prophesied in thy name? and in thy name have cast out devils? and in thy name done many wonderful works? [23] And then will I profess unto them, I never knew you: depart from me, ye that work iniquity. (Mat 7: 21-23)

See the key phrase is: "he that doeth the will of my Father in heaven", and so what is the will of the heavenly Father? This is going to be the real shocker to many. If you really want to know what the will of the heavenly Father is? Then you should learn the Pentateuch or the Torah, the first five books in the scriptures. That is His will because that will be the way it is going to be in the eternal home. See things will be going His way not mans! He is the creator the maker of all, the one we owe all our praise to, He is the one that formed man from the earth and made all that is was and ever will be! "HalleluYah." And so it will be a joy to us to be obedient to Him and His ways, I will also say if we cannot do His will here what makes any of us think we will even be there with Him! Yahushua is our atonement so we can have favor and forgiveness of sins, and become obedient to Him and His word, and desires for our life eternal. Yahushua did not give all for us to become cleansed in heart so we can walk into heaven thinking we do not have to be obedient to the Fathers will. That would be a terrible- thing to try to walk into the heavenly place and hear Yahushua say "be away with you!" You are only His if you are doing the will of the Father in Heaven, YHWH none other.

[46] While he yet talked to the people, behold, his mother
and his brethren stood without, desiring to speak with
him. [47] Then one said unto him, Behold, thy mother and
thy brother stand without, desiring to speak with thee. [48]
But he answered and said unto him that told him, Who is
my mother? and who are my brethren? [49] And he stretched
forth his hand toward his disciples, and said, Behold my
mother and my brethren! [50] For whosoever shall do the will
of my Father which is in heaven, the same is my brother,
and sister, and mother. (Mat 12:46-50)

Make no mistake, those that are lead by the spirit that teaches otherwise is of (another) Messiah. And is a deception because plainly you can see if you disregard the

Fathers will you will not enter into the kingdom of heaven because Yahushua is the door keeper and none will enter in whom He does not know!

[6] This parable spake Yahushua unto them: but they understood not what things they were which he spake unto them. [7] Then said Yahushua unto them again, Verily, verily, I say unto you, I am the door of the sheep. [8] All that ever came before me are thieves and robbers: but the sheep did not hear them. [9] I am the door: by me if any man enter in, he shall be saved, and shall go in and out, and find pasture. [10] The thief cometh not, but for to steal, and to kill, and to destroy: I am come that they might have life, and that they might have it more abundantly. [11] I am the good shepherd: the good shepherd giveth his life for the sheep. (John 10:6-11)

Those He does not know by the will of the Father YHWH will not enter in to the door. All the others had been deceived and kept from this real truth so they would not have life. This is a deception of satan the angel of false light, whom also has ministers of false righteousness as well and scripture verifies.

[12] But what I do, that I will do, that I may cut off occasion from them which desire occasion; that wherein they glory, they may be found even as we. [13] For such are false apostles, deceitful workers, transforming themselves into the apostles of Messiah. [14] And no marvel; for satan himself is transformed into an angel of light. [15] Therefore it is no great thing if his ministers also be transformed

as the ministers of righteousness; whose end shall be according to their works. (2Cor 11:12-15)

Any minister that is against the Messiah Yahushua and uses the scriptures of YHWH, whom does not keep the heavenly Fathers Sabbath, but lifts up another messiah this one is in the true anti – messiah spirit. That spirit has lead people to everlasting death, these are the ones that are deceivers and thieves, original wolves in sheep's clothing. Many of them steal from their own flocks out of evil intentions and covetousness. Remember the word says do not steal and those who steal from another man or woman for personal gain or false reasons will not live or enter into the kingdom of heaven. Also the word says do not cause a sister or a brother to sin for it will not be well with thee. Those ministers do not even know the Father and so are unable to love him. Those who steal from their neighbor do not love them. And if they teach others to do likewise they are sending others to their death.

[19] Whosoever therefore shall break one of these least commandments, and shall teach men so, he shall be called the least in the kingdom of heaven: but whosoever shall do and teach them, the same shall be called great in the kingdom of heaven. [20] For I say unto you, That except your righteousness shall exceed the righteousness of the scribes and Pharisees, ye shall in no case enter into the kingdom of heaven. (Mat 5:19-20)

That truly only applies to those whom Yahushua let in through the door and not anti-messiah's. Think not that you can find a loop hole YHWH made His way in Yahushua fail safe! Because Yahushua Ha Mashiyach is the door keeper and will reign on the throne for ever, HalleluYah! Now if you ask does this mean I have to keep the law, then why did Messiah die for me? Go back and read the previous pages of this writing and your questions should be answered. Now if you say do we stone adulterer and adulteress, the answer is no! The scriptures clearly state we are to be obedient to those ruling powers over us in the nation we are in, for YHWH allows those to be in place for His reasons. Because the real true way of salvation is in Yahushua Ha Mashiyach, and He himself kept all the Torah because He had the spirit of love and obedience. This is what we ourselves are being called to become obedient sons and daughters in YHWH.

[14] For as many as are led by the Spirit of Elohim, they are the sons of Elohim. [15] For ye have not received the spirit of bondage again to fear; but ye have received the Spirit of adoption, whereby we cry, Abba, Father. [16] The Spirit itself beareth witness with our spirit, that we are the children of Elohim: [17] And if children, then heirs; heirs of YHWH, and joint-heirs with Mashiyach; if so be that we suffer with him, that we may be also glorified together. [18] For I reckon that the sufferings of this present time are not worthy to be compared with the glory which shall be revealed in us. [19]

For the earnest expectation of the creature waiteth for the manifestation of the sons of YHWH. (Rom 8:14-19)

John 1: [10] He was in the world, and the world was made by him, and the world knew him not. [11] He came unto his own, and his own received him not. [12] But as many as received him, to them gave he power to become the sons of YHWH, even to them that believe on his name: [13] Which were born, not of blood, nor of the will of the flesh, nor of the will of man, but of YHWH. (John 1:10-13)

[14] Be ye not unequally yoked together with unbelievers: for what fellowship hath righteousness with unrighteousness? and what communion hath light with darkness?

[15] And what concord hath Messiah with Belial? or what part hath he that believeth with an infidel? [16] And what agreement hath the temple of YHWH with idols? for ye are the temple of the living Elohim; as YHWH hath said, I will dwell in them, and walk in them; and I will be their Elohim, and they shall be my people. [17] Wherefore come out from among them, and be ye separate, saith Yahweh of Host, and touch not the unclean thing; and I will receive you, [18] And will be a Father unto you, and ye shall be my sons and daughters, saith Yahweh Most High.(2Cor 6:14-18)

[3] Even so we, when we were children, were in bondage under the elements of the world:

[4] But when the fullness of the time was come, YHWH sent forth his Son, made of a woman, made under the law, [5] To redeem them that were under the law, that we might

receive the adoption of sons. [6] And because ye are sons, YHWH hath sent forth the Spirit of his Son into your hearts, crying, Abba, Father. [7] Wherefore thou art no more a servant, but a son; and if a son, then an heir of YHWH through Messiah. (Gal 4:3-7)

We ourselves can overcome once the spirit of adoption is with in our temples. This is the real purpose of YHWH's working through His Son Yahushua so we can become sons as He is.

[1] Behold, what manner of love the Father hath bestowed upon us, that we should be called the sons of YHWH: therefore the world knoweth us not, because it knew him not.

[2] Beloved, now are we the sons of Elohim, and it doth not yet appear what we shall be: but we know that, when he shall appear, we shall be like him; for we shall see him as he is. (1John 3:1-2)

[7] He that overcometh shall inherit all things; and I will be his Elohim, and he shall be my son. (Rev 21:7)

Now the scriptures do not lie, or even contradict it self like many imply. But it does verify and validate our existence in the eternal place with our creator and heavenly Father YHWH. The reason we are to become as sons? We are all His creation and made in His likeness for just that reason, we are all to become spirit beings, as He is we are to become. He uses the term sons because we are all His children, and it makes our relationship valid and accomplished with Him even before we walk in with Him. Remember He knows the beginning from the end. We are all called to obedience of YHWH's word and way, many say we are set free from the Torah but all the law and the prophets hang on the Torah. Torah meaning (instruction of righteousness) Yahushua gave His blood and life as our sacrifice taking upon Himself all our iniquities and shame, to complete the Spirit of Torah in us, all who believe and call upon His name. When we first walk into the truth and His spirit of righteousness we all are filled with the love of Yahushua the changing power of overcoming all our hurts and pains. Because the power of His love overcomes all things, as it is written:

Proverbs 10:[12] Hatred stirreth up strifes: but love covereth all sins.

This is a part of walking in the babe syndrome, when we become learned and taught, in the scriptures and ways of YHWH. This is a learning process we all go through whom come in later in our lives. But as we learn and become cleansed it is more apparent to us obedience is a requirement and condition of our salvation. Love and obedience are required for us to learn and continue learning His word, which is the process of applying what we are taught from the scriptures.

[19] Now we know that what things soever the law saith, it saith to them who are under the law: that every mouth may be stopped, and all the world may become guilty before

YHWH. [20] Therefore by the deeds of the law there shall no
flesh be justified in his sight: for by the (law / Torah) is the
knowledge of sin. [21] But now the righteousness of Elohim
without the law is manifested, being witnessed by the law
and the prophets; [22] Even the righteousness of YHWH
which is by faith of Yahushua Ha Mashiyach unto all and
upon all them that believe: for there is no difference: [23] For
all have sinned, and come short of the glory of YHWH; [24]
Being justified freely by his grace through the redemption
that is in Yahushua Ha Mashiyach: [25] Whom Elohim hath
set forth to be a propitiation through faith in his blood, to
declare his righteousness for the remission of sins that are
past, through the forbearance of Elohim; [26] To declare, at
this time his righteousness: that he might be just, and the
justifier of him which believeth in Yahushua. [27] Where is
boasting then? It is excluded. By what law? of works? Nay:
but by the law of faith. [28] Therefore we conclude that a man
is justified by faith without the deeds of the law. [29] Is he the
El of the Jews only? is he not also of the Gentiles? Yes, of the
Gentiles also: [30] Seeing it is one Elohim, which shall justify
the circumcision by faith, and uncircumcision through
faith. [31] Do we then make void the Torah through faith?
Yah forbid: yea, we establish the Torah. (Rom 3:19-31)

That is not the only scripture that explains what Yahushua is relaying to us through the apostles writings about obedience.

1 Therefore thou art inexcusable, O man, whosoever thou art that judgest: for whcrein thou judgest another, thou condemnest thyself; for thou that judgest doest the samc things. 2 But we are sure that the judgment of Elohim is according to truth against them which commit such things. 3 And thinkest thou this, O man, that judgest them which do such things, and doest the same, that thou shalt escape the judgment of YHWH? 4 Or despisest thou the riches of his goodness and forbearance and longsuffering; not knowing that the goodness of YHWH leadeth thee to repentance? 5 But after thy hardness and impenitent heart treasurest up unto thyself wrath against the day of wrath and revelation of the righteous judgment of Elohim; 6 Who will render to every man according to his deeds: 7 To them who by patient continuance in well doing seek for glory and honour and immortality, eternal life: 8 But unto them that are contentious, and do not obey the truth, but obey unrighteousness, indignation and wrath, 9 Tribulation and anguish, upon every soul of man that doeth evil, of the Jew first, and also of the Gentile; 10 But glory, honour, and peace, to every man that worketh good, to the Jew first, and also to the Gentile: 11 For there is no respect of persons with Yahweh. 12 For as many as have sinned without law shall also perish without law: and as many as have sinned in the law shall be judged by the law; 13 (For not the hearers of the law are just before Elohim, but the doers of the (law / Torah) shall be justified. 14 For when the Gentiles, which

have not the law, do by nature the things contained in the law, these, having not the law, are a law unto themselves: [15] Which shew the work of the law written in their hearts, their conscience also bearing witness, and their thoughts the mean while accusing or else excusing one another;) [16] In the day when Elohim shall judge the secrets of men by Yahushua Ha Mashiyach according to my gospel. (Rom 2:1-16)

17 Only, as Elohim has given to each one, as the Master has called each one, so let him walk. And so I order in all the assemblies. 18Was anyone called while circumcised? Let him not become uncircumcised. Was anyone called while uncircumcised? Let him not be circumcised. 19The circumcision is nothing, and the uncircumcision is nothing, but the keeping of the commandments of YHWH is of value. (1Cor 7:17-19)

Romans 10:[1] Brethren, my heart's desire and prayer to YHWH for Yisrael is, that they might be saved. [2] For I bear them record that they have a zeal of Elohim, but not according to knowledge. [3] For they being ignorant of Elohim's righteousness, and going about to establish their own righteousness, have not submitted themselves unto the righteousness of YHWH. [4] For Messiah is the goal of the law / Torah for righteousness to every one that believeth. (Rom 10:1-4)

Strong's meaning of (goal /end): G5056 telos- tel'-os, tello's; (to set out for a definite point or goal); translates as "end,"custom, "uttermost, "finally, "ending" once, and "by (one's) continual. 1 end. 1A termination, the limit at which a thing ceases to be (always of the end of some act or state, but not of the end of a period of time). 1B the end. 1B1 the last in any succession or series. 1B2 eternal. 1C that by which a thing is finished, its close, issue. 1D the end to which all things relate, the aim, purpose. 2 toll, custom (i.e. indirect tax on goods).

It is clear we are to establish the law or Torah of righteousness in our walk with Him, keeping in mind the Torah is the will of the Father, and none will be justified without His Torah of righteousness in their hearts. (Mat 7:21-23). Let's look on this wisely, to become a son we must walk in the spirit of love and righteousness, which leads us into obedience and helps us overcome the ways and evils of the world. WOW what a great deal that is. Not to mention the fact of eternal life and we are all to be sons, heirs of salvation with the Father YHWH, by the true and awesome name of the beloved Son Yahushua Ha Mashiyach! HalleluYah! So you might say does this mean I have to follow the (Old Testament)? of course you do have to keep the Fathers word in obedience to His will. The Ten Commandments are His will as Torah or law is the principles of right doing and proper knowledge of right and wrong. If you read the first 5 books in the Bible you will see it is all shadow pictures of the eternal place. Those are the rules of what not to do and what is going to be accepted as proper conduct. Love your neighbor as your self, but first and utmost Love YHWH with all your heart, mind, soul, and strength. These principles will all be closely guarded and done by all. But the one that will completely boggle those who know not His Torah is the keeping of the feasts and His Sabbath. All things will be done by all who are in the eternal kingdom because it is His word. YHWH also says He changes not, remember that! But the reason for the analogy of sons is obedience and love. Because a son obeys and loves his father and wants to do everything that is pleasing to his father, for acceptance and validation of the one whom he is fashioned after. We all as children seek to do well in our parents eyes, we always seek their approval and acknowledgement of a job well done. Almost all of us at one time or another seek positive reinforcement from our parents, because this makes us feel accepted and loved when we hear words of encouragement. You can see the similarities and can realize many times YHWH uses the relationship between a father and a son to explain His plight with us. I use the word plight because most often than not we are almost always hard to deal with, and our Heavenly Father YHWH is in it for the long haul not just a fleeting moment. We are to become spiritual beings, this man is temporal the spirit is eternal. As in all things YHWH follows His own word of truth to save us and help us to become as He is.

[12] For the word of YHWH is quick, and powerful, and sharper than any two edged sword, piercing even to the dividing asunder of soul and spirit, and of the joints and

marrow, and is a discerner of the thoughts and intents of the heart. (Heb 4:12)

The power of His word is of divine magnitude and beyond our full capacity of understanding because it transforms us into spiritual people.

[63] It is the spirit that quickeneth; the flesh profiteth nothing: the words that I speak unto you, they are spirit, and they are life. [64] But there are some of you that believe not. For Yahushua knew from the beginning who they were that believed not, and who should betray him. [65] And he said, There fore said I unto you, that no man can come unto me, except it were given unto him of my Father. (John 6:63-65)

So by the power of His word we are transformed or even learning to conform to His ways. I have seen the power of His word in action many times, it is awesome and breathtaking to say the least. Almost every time I have seen the Spirit move in power, a step of obedience was first done. It takes an act of obedience for the power of the Spirit to move on the speaking of His word. Those of you who have been involved with the Spirit moving in power know what that means. And others who desire that, must learn from the teacher Yahushua how this is accomplished, remember He is the teacher in our souls, those who are born again and of water and of spirit. (John 3:3 + 3:5)

[1] Now Naaman, captain of the host of the king of Syria, was a great man with his master, and honourable, because by him YHWH had given deliverance unto Syria: he was

also a mighty man in valour, but he was a leper. [2] And
the Syrians had gone out by companies, and had brought
away captive out of the land of Israel a little maid; and she
waited on Naaman's wife. [3] And she said unto her mistress,
Would YHWH my Master were with the prophet that is
in Samaria! for he would recover him of his leprosy. [4] And
one went in, and told his lord, saying, Thus and thus said
the maid that is of the land of Israel. [5] And the king of
Syria said, Go to, go, and I will send a letter unto the king
of Israel. And he departed, and took with him ten talents
of silver, and six thousand pieces of gold, and ten changes
of raiment. [6] And he brought the letter to the king of Israel,
saying, Now when this letter is come unto thee, behold, I
have therewith sent Naaman my servant to thee, that thou
mayest recover him of his leprosy. [7] And it came to pass,
when the king of Israel had read the letter, that he rent
his clothes, and said, Am I Elohim, to kill and to make
alive, that this man doth send unto me to recover a man of
his leprosy? wherefore consider, I pray you, and see how he
seeketh a quarrel against me. [8] And it was so, when Elisha
the man of YHWH had heard that the king of Israel had
rent his clothes, that he sent to the king, saying, Wherefore
hast thou rent thy clothes? let him come now to me, and he
shall know that there is a prophet in Israel. [9] So Naaman
came with his horses and with his chariot, and stood at the
door of the house of Elisha. [10] And Elisha sent a messenger
unto him, saying, Go and wash in Jordan seven times, and

thy flesh shall come again to thee, and thou shalt be clean. 11
But Naaman was wroth, and went away, and said, Behold, I
thought, He will surely come out to me, and stand, and call
on the name of YHWH his Elohim, and strike his hand
over the place, and recover the leper. 12 Are not Abana and
Pharpar, rivers of Damascus, better than all the waters of
Israel? may I not wash in them, and be clean? So he turned
and went away in a rage. 13 And his servants came near, and
spake unto him, and said, My father, if the prophet had
bid thee do some great thing, wouldest thou not have done
it? how much rather then, when he saith to thee, Wash,
and be clean? 14 Then went he down, and dipped himself
seven times in Jordan, according to the saying of the man
of YHWH: and his flesh came again like unto the flesh of
a little child, and he was clean. (2Kings 5:1-14)

If Naaman would not have been obedient he would not have been healed, I do realize he bawked but the final decision to be obedient was what was needed. That is why I used this particular story from the scriptures because we might make a mistake then finally do as He requested then we get our desired outcome, the key is not giving up. Obedience is required in any case when desiring the mighty move of the Spirit for healings, miracles, and mighty manifestations of signs and wonders. Only as sons of the most high are we able to be apart of these things as Yahushua the Messiah uses us to heal and speak into peoples lives, the things He desires for them. It is an important fact, we must be obedient. Son ship is a very clear way to look at the relationship we have with the Father YHWH through the Son Yahushua the Messiah, YHWH's beloved. Every day is a new day in the Master Yahushua and every day is a blessed day of learning the way. More and more wonderful things are taught us by His word when we seek His knowledge and receive the relational insight of the scriptures. This is were we all need to be daily in the word, learning every day some new thing or revelations and truth. Some times we think we are doing good and find out maybe we were wrong, for instance. I am an American citizen well the scriptures are from the Hebrew tongue, and has been translated into other languages for understanding of His word. So I tell you these things not to make any one stumble but to learn and not to offend either. You see the word Lord is a Phoenician word used to call an other deity.

H1168[*Ba'al* –bah'al] n.pr, m loc. Same as 1167: translates as Baal 62, times- Baalim 18 times; *1 supreme male divinity of the Phoenicians or Canaanites. 2 a Reubenite.* 3 the son of Jehiel and grandfather of Saul. 4 a town of Simeon, probably identical to Baalath-beer. *Additional Information: Baal = "lord".* Also H1167[baʿal-*bah'-al]*n.m. from 1166; 82 occurrences, translates as "man" 25 times, "owner" 14 times, "husband" 11 times, "have" seven times, "master" five times, "man given" twice, "adversary" once, "archers" once, "babbler + 3956" once, "bird + 3671" once, "captain" once, "confederate + 1285" once, and translated miscellaneously

12 times. 1 owner, husband, lord. 1a owner. 1b a husband. 1c citizens, inhabitants. *1d rulers, lords. 1e (noun of relationship used to characterise—ie, master of dreams). 1f lord (used of foreign gods).*

Now you can see the terminology of the word lord and the reason many will not use that way of speaking as talking to the heavenly Father. And truly His name is not ba al or rah or bah al it is YHWH ,Yahweh of Hosts the Most High as the Sons true name is Yahushua which means YHWH is salvation. Many people say what is in a name it does not matter, but I assure you it really does make a difference. If He did not want anyone to know or speak his name why did YHWH have it written in the scriptures almost 7000 times alone? Because the name depicts the character of the person and or their identity. Just like the term god that has no bearing or direction since it does not make a claim to the most high YHWH, it is only a title not a name and can have reference to any mans false deity. For instance: the term god comes from the name gad which means:

H1171 [Ba 'al Gad] bah 'al gawd)- n.pr.loc. from 1168 and 1409; three occurrences, translates as "Baalgad" three times. 1 a city noted for Baal-worship, located at the most northern or northwestern point to which Joshua's victories extended. Additional Information: Baal-gad = "lord of fortune".

It may be hard to except when you use these terminologies but it is all a slight subtle deception that has been perpetrated on those believing on His word. There is a history behind the scriptures even making it into the common mans hand. For over the 2000 years, it is said over 500 million people have died for the keeping of His scriptures. The history is absolutely amazing and a powerful testimony of the Yahweh's love for His people, and all they had to truly go through just to have the scriptures copied. In any case we need to understand there has been many different discrepancies in the remaking of the scriptures going way back to the first translation from the Hebrew writings.

Many are just due, to the understanding of that particular culture or of the translator, and many have been deceptions to the following generations because of lack of knowledge. Fore instance the word lord is a Phoenician terminology of which they called there deity ba'al. That is an example of what I was talking of how words deceive, from one generation to the next. In all the scriptures they are about the same stories and prophetic writings, but have been altered in some cases, to accommodate their doctrinal belief. I will also say complacency is very common in today's belief systems. Many do not pursue the true meanings or words for knowledge of the scriptures. We as believers should search diligently for truth and ways of messiah, we should ask for truth every day in our prayer time. Then follow His lead and search out what He shows us and has others tell us as well. He uses other believers to tell us something we are not aware of yet. I have even had some worldly people say things I know was from the direction of the Holy Father Yah, to fill in the blanks at times. In any case we are to search out the true meanings and revelations of YHWH's word for our own understanding and increase of His knowledge in our hearts and souls. For instance the apostolic writings they are about Messiah and also our obedience to the Fathers will, many do not see this because of teachings that appose the true way and light. Many are very subtle and hard to notice but in the long run they are very costly as you will see.

[1] Whosoever believeth that Yahushua is the Messiah is born of YHWH: and every one that loveth him that begat loveth him also that is begotten of him.

[2] By this we know that we love the children of Elohim,
when we love YHWH and keep his commandments. 3 For
this is the love of YHWH, that we keep his commandments:
and his commandments are not grievous. (1John 5:1-3)

Now I realize this is an apostolic writing, that has been written by an apostle of the anointed savior Yahushua the Messiah, there is no argument with that but this also is a verification of the Torah. Some may say law but it is the instruction of righteousness, is it not?

1 My little children, these things write I unto you, that
ye sin not. And if any man sin, we have an advocate with
the Father, the Messiah Yahushua the righteous: 2 And he

is the propitiation for our sins: and not for ours only, but also for the sins of the whole world.

3 And hereby we do know that we know him, if we keep his commandments. 4 He that saith, I know him, and keepeth not his commandments, is a liar, and the truth is not in him. 5 But whoso keepeth his word, in him verily is the love of Elohim perfected: hereby know we that we are in him. 6 He that saith he abideth in him ought himself also so to walk, even as he walked. (1John 2:1-6)

There is no way that can be explained except we must keep the commandments that are in the Torah, you see we are unable to pick the parts we like and disregard the rest, that is making a mockery of His word, and it is also wrong. Anyone can turn the verses by taking things out of context, and inserting their own understanding. But hear this, those who give false understanding to those they teach have a hidden agenda or underlined reason for disregarding the true desire of YHWH. Back in the ancient times religion was used as a catalyst to control the masses. The Roman Catholic churches would read the scriptures to the layman in Latin, a language they did not know. John Wycliffe was one of the first pioneers of translating the bible into English so the average plow hand could come to the saving knowledge of the truth, and just so you know the Roman Catholic leaders forbid the translating of the scriptures. And John Wycliffe was eventually acussed by the Roman Catholic church leaders, for heresy, and many of the believers that followed him in the belief were burnt at the steak with their scriptures hanging around their necks. Because it was law, that was about the inquisition. Because the inquisition was not about witchcraft, but putting the bible believing groups that did not agree with the catholic papacy's to an end. The truth be known they hunted bible believers who did not partake of the catholic way.

(Source: From the Television Documentary)

A Lamp in the Dark: The Untold History of the Bible An exciting documentary that unfolds the fascinating untold history of the Bible, revealing critical information often overlooked in modern histories. Enter into a world of saints and martyrs battling against spies, assassins and wolves in sheep's clothing.

Throughout the Middle Ages, the Papal Inquisition forbade biblical translation, threatening imprisonment and death to those who disobeyed. Learn the stories of valiant warriors of the faith, such as John Wycliffe, William Tyndale, Martin Luther, the ancient Waldenses, Albigenses and others who hazarded their lives for the sake of sharing the Gospel light with a world drowning in darkness. Once the common people were able to read the Bible, the world was turned upside down through the Protestant Reformation.

The Reformers subdued whole kingdoms by preaching the grace of God, and exposing the unbiblical doctrines of Rome. In response, the Vatican would launch a Counter

Reformation to destroy the work of the Reformers, including the bibles they produced.

This video covers subjects ranging from the Gospels, to the Reformation with Martin Luther, the Counter-Reformation and the Jesuits (the Black Pope and Sovereign Military Order of the Knights of Malta), and the fascinating story surrounding William Tyndale and the different Bible translations .http://topdocumentaryfilms.com/a-lamp-in-the-dark-the-untold-history-of-the-bible/

1 Therefore thou art inexcusable, O man, whosoever
thou art that judgest: for wherein thou judgest another, thou
condemnest thyself; for thou that judgest doest the same
things. 2 But we are sure that the judgment of YHWH is
according to truth against them which commit such things.
3 And thinkest thou this,

O man, that judgest them which do such things, and
doest the same, that thou shalt escape the judgment of
YHWH? 4 Or despisest thou the riches of his goodness
and forbearance and longsuffering; not knowing that the
goodness of YHWH leadeth thee to repentance? 5 But
after thy hardness and impenitent heart treasurest up unto
thyself wrath against the day of wrath and revelation of
the righteous judgment of YHWH; 6 Who will render
to every man according to his deeds: 7 To them who by
patient continuance in well doing seek for glory and
honour and immortality, eternal life: 8 But unto them
that are contentious, and do not obey the Torah, but obey

unrighteousness, indignation and wrath, 9 Tribulation and anguish, upon every soul of man that doeth evil, of the Jew first, and also of the Gentile; 10

But glory, honour, and peace, to every man that worketh good, to the Jew first, and also to the Gentile: 11 For there is no respect of persons with YHWH. 12 For as many as have sinned without Torah shall also perish without Torah: and as many as have sinned in the Torah shall be judged by the Torah; 13 (For not the hearers of the (law or Torah) shall be justified before YHWH, but the doers of the (law or Torah) shall be justified. (Rom 2:1-13)

Again it does come down to the choice of being obedient, according to the scriptures. Did Messiah lay down His life for those who will in the end disregard the will of the heavenly Father? I should think not, but on the contrary, we are to become completely obedient to the desires of the heavenly father, according to His word.

We are to be obedient sons of YHWH in Yahushua Ha Mashiyach.

Romans 3: 31 Do we then make void the law / Torah through faith? YHWH forbid: yea, we establish the law.

To establish the Torah or law, that is what Yahushua gave all for, for us to be able to become complete, the fulfillment of the Torah in each and every one of us.

He came unto His own and they received Him not, but as many as did receive Him to them gave He the power to become sons of the Most High El YHWH, to them that believed on His name. (John 1:11-12)

It is a marvelous thing, we that believe and walk in His word get to become sons of YHWH, why because we are learning of Him to be come obedient to His ways.

We must not be so arrogant to think the creator of the whole earth is going to do it our way? But as the old saying goes, it is my way or the highway. This is the reason for the Torah the will of the Father YHWH, so we can know Him by His word, YHWH says I am YHWH I change not.

Any one who thinks they have it all good and worked out with Him but does not know His word or ways, will not make it, because they will not know Him, they will only know of Him and miss the mark, the true goal of the scriptures. That is to teach us to become like Him so we can have that fellowship with Him in perfect love and worship. This happens when we are in the Son Yahushua, and are obedient to the will of the Father.

Yahushua set us free so we could be like him, sons of the Most High Yahweh. This also brings to mind the reason for the perfect order of YHWH, for our eternal lives with him.

Society today has changed the truth, and are making lite, His word of life, by making it mean another thing than it's true intent, even changing the words. I was walking by a catholic school church in Tulsa, Oklahoma and noticed the commandments on the front of the building, there were only nine, they had left out – Do not make unto thee any graven image, or any likeness of any thing that is in heaven above, or that is in the earth beneath, or that is in the water under the earth: – (Ex 20 :4) I do not think they forgot to put it up their, I just think they disregard that particular command, other wise it would be up on that building. As funny as that sounds, this is the reason many will suffer and not make it, total disregard for the real truth. That is disobedience to the Fathers word and way. Not to mention changing His scriptures, just like one word in a paragraph changed creates a whole new meaning, so does leaving parts out. If we disregard His word, we disregard the one who sent it, the Heavenly Father Yahweh. Yahushua made that clear to us all.

[23] That all men should honour the Son, even as they honour the Father. He that honoureth not the Son honoureth not the Father which hath sent him. [24] Verily, verily, I say unto you, He that heareth my word, and believeth on him that sent me, hath everlasting life, and shall not come into condemnation; but is passed from death unto life. (John 5:23-24)

See the importance of receiving the word which the Father had spoken to us through Moses and the prophets, and especially the words of our savior the Messiah Yahushua.

Here is a good way to look at it, the first five books are the Torah or law, the will of the Father, then the prophets the words of YHWH's heart spoken through the servant of YHWH. First correction, love, guidance then drawing us back, these are His ways in calling use back when we make mistakes. And it has always been in love yes love, because He only corrects a son of His love, all the times the prophets said words hard for the children to bear, they were condemned because of their own wrong doing. They would rise up and attack, and many times over, killed the prophets.

37 O Jerusalem, Jerusalem, thou that killest the prophets,
and stonest them which are sent unto thee, how often would I have gathered thy children together, even as a hen gathereth her chickens under her wings, and ye would not! (Mat 23:37)

The scriptures tell us the Pharisees and Sadducees, those who where the spiritual leaders of that time, would have the prophets put to death one way or another. Because they were not doing as the Father YHWH said in His word. Every time the prophets spoke to them, His word would completely convict them. Messiah was put to death by them as was the prophets before His time. This is a repeat of what we know has happened again and again, this day and age it still goes on. But because of today's times and the laws of man it is not as open or as well known because of the lack of believers today. Back then everyone believed in a most high Elohim of some kind, but because of there mind set many turned away because they thought their El had forsaken them. Most were turned away by the religious leaders of that time period. With every time period there was change in mankind, the worldly ways never stood still. The Pharisees and Sadducees made religious decisions that made many fall and stumble. Things aren't that different from today's religious leaders, they still do the same things as in Yahushua's day. I say that because the biggest majority of the modern day ministers in the U.S.A are still teaching and preaching doctrines of man and not teaching how to do the will of the Heavenly Father YHWH. Remember Yahushua did not come to set free the religious leaders but to reprove them and correct the wrongs they had burdened the people under.

17 Think not that I am come to destroy the law, or the
prophets: I am not come to destroy, but to fulfil. 18 For verily
I say unto you, Till heaven and earth pass, one jot or one
tittle shall in no wise pass from the law, till all be fulfilled.

19 Whosoever therefore shall break one of these least
commandments, and shall teach men so, he shall be called
the least in the kingdom of heaven: but whosoever shall
do and teach them, the same shall be called great in the
kingdom of heaven. 20 For I say unto you, That except your
righteousness shall exceed the righteousness of the scribes
and Pharisees, ye shall in no case enter into the kingdom of
heaven. (Mat 5:17-20)

Yahushua had to correct them all, every time He was in public they would try to trick Him in the Torah, as to make Him look foolish. But His answers bewildered the religious leaders and scribes. They could not contend with Yahushua in the scriptures because He always had an answer that corrected them in that day. Many ministers in today's religious settings do not openly study the Torah or law as they call it, because it makes light of the wrongs they are doing. Now in this day and times the average family goes to a church where they like the pastor or leaders. It is as though the criteria is about the pastor and if he does what you want or like for him to do and preach. Well I will say this, the church or it's pastor will not save you, and cannot. The reason? We are to look to Him that saves, not man and mans ways. You must have the relationship with Yahushua Ha Mashiyach, the beloved of YHWH the Father. Today there are thousands and thousands of churches across the nation some small and some large. Each one of those leaders are teaching the doctrine they have been taught by another man, who was taught by another man, ect. Many of the population in this nation do not know the man's doctrine is death not life, it is a deception of the real way. Here is the proof, Roman Catholicism, is the tree of all Christianity today. Roman Catholicism was started by Constantine he is the one who made Catholicism the world religion after his rise to power. And he was at first a follower of the pagan way and religious ceremonies, he was a leader in the black arts, a cult leader or as we would say to day in (paganism). Constantine also made himself a religious leader after he made Roman Catholicism the world wide religion. Now this was just the beginning of what was to become of Christianity. It was the Catholic church that went out and killed the believers, by the orders of the popes. Because other believers did not partake of the catholic ways, or their sacraments. It was also during this time the term Christians began to come into play, about 316-320 AD or so. The Roman Catholic priest and pope made an edict that all the Jews would have to put yellow stars on their clothing to identify them as Jews. Constantine also sent out an edict that made Sunday the first day of the week the official day of worship, because the Romans and all their forefathers kept that day all the way back to Nimrod and the tower of babble. Constantine also sent out and edict telling all the people, (if anyone was keeping the Sabbath or the feasts YHWH had written in the scriptures, that person or family would be put to death). It was said the priest were so zealous about that edict, when the weather was cold they would go to the highest building or cliffs and watch to see which houses did not have smoke coming out of the chimney on YHWH's Sabbath. If they had none they went and attacked them, ripping them out of their houses and burning them at the steak. It was also said that many of the Jews and their families snuck out in the middle of the night, and went to far away lands. This is and was the beginning of christianity, at first the Catholics called them Christians to be an insult to the Jewish people, that was in the days of Constantine about (316, AD) before that the true believers in Messiah were called followers of the "WAY" or Messianic. Now keep in mind there were many Jewish believers in YHWH that did not believe on the Messiah, which is where many of the negative writings concerning the Jewish people came from. The catholics wrote many bad things about the Jewish based on the claims of the followers of YHWH who did not believe the Messiah had come yet. Many rabbis and religious leaders were blind to the truth after Messiah Ascended because they had not ministered as YHWH desired. But did according to mans way the works of the flesh in the law, and did not minister in love or truth. This is another reason why the rabbis had been given over to their own ways because they them selves disregarded the scriptures, YHWH's words, for the word of man. A perfect example is the Talmud, also many writings of the Midrash which are both called commentaries of law and scriptures as described in American dictionaries. It is a fact the carnal mind cannot see the heart of the spirit or it's true intent, because the carnal man is at war with the spirit of life, because they that are carnal are in death and not life. And even a very smart man cannot conceive or understand the workings of the Spirit. Also those in the wrong spirit will not and cannot see properly. This is one reason there are so many false doctrines in the masses of believers world wide. It is also a fact the Catholic popes, and leaders took the scriptures of YHWH and the Apostolic writings and made them their own, in all realization they committed (replacement theology). This is why the names of the Father and the Names of the Son were changed or taken out, because they were not the names the Romans used in their worship. They used the names zues, jove, jupiture, and others and many of the scriptures reflect this fact because of the names they use instead of YHWH and Yahushua. Much of this was the work of the Jesuits, a secret organization that was considered an assassins guild and a dutiful organization of the Catholic popes. It has been said they went to the farthest extremes to eliminate the writings and meanings of truth in other believers, or followers of Messiah Yahushua, infiltrating them, to find out what they new and practiced, then brought them in if they were not loyal to the catholic papacy. Then the leaders would have them burnt at the steak with there scriptures around their necks. It is also a fact the King James Version scriptures was one of the best translations of the Hebrew and Aramaic writings. Although almost every name in the KJV was changed and hence forth diluted, this was also a deception of the Jesuits, and Roman Catholics. For instance a name identifies you as who you are, when you go to another country or place where you are not known they will greet you and ask your name. You then in turn learn theirs but you answer to yours and they answer to theirs. They will not call you by any other name, nor will you call them by another name. Because that is who you are, do you say the real names and meanings in the scriptures? If you go into another country and introduce your self, after a long time they say here is the same meaning for your name in our language. You then allow them to use that name, but when you write a check will that check get cashed in that foreign name at your bank, no it is not you, to them it is a forgery,

This is the same meaning for the anti- Messiah the word for that is an other, there really is no sense in using the term anti- christ because that is not His but an other. That term truly means an imposter or false Messiah, one who mimics the real one and deceives many, this was already here in the Apostles times, as many wrote of them especially John the brother of Yahushua the true Messiah.

17 And the world passeth away, and the lust thereof:
but he that doeth the will of YHWH abideth for ever. 18
Little children, it is the last time: and as ye have heard that
antichrist shall come, even now are there many antichrists
or anti messiah's; whereby we know that it is the last time.
19 They went out from us, but they were not of us; for if they
had been of us, they would no doubt have continued with
us: but they went out, that they might be made manifest
that they were not all of us. (1John 2:17-19)

What that truly means is an imposter, another one who mimics the real messiah. Keep this in mind also the term anti Messiah was the term used not Christ. That is the spirit of deception, the spirit that does mimic the real Messiah, but deceives by not leading them to real and complete scriptural truth. This is why we must go beyond what the teachers say, and look for our selves, seek the real truth, ask in prayer for the real true way. The anti Messiah spirit will not reveal complete scriptural knowledge so as to turn the believers away from the real Messiah.

John 5: [39] Search the scriptures; for in them ye think ye have eternal life: and they are they which testify of me. [40] And ye will not come to me, that ye might have life. [41] I receive not honour from men. [42] But I know you, that ye have not the love of Elohim in you. [43] I am come in my Father's name, and ye receive me not: if another shall come in his own name, him ye will receive. (John 5:39-43)

See the scriptures tell of Him and His coming, the words of Moses and the prophets both spoke of Him, as did the Psalms. So how can anyone know this unless they study the whole Bible? It is fact! All the things written in the Messianic writings or what is called the New Testament is of the Mosaic word, written by Moses, and the prophets. I had a united Pentecostal Minister say to me, it is not wise to teach from the Old Testament, because the people ask questions you cannot answer! Then he said when you do many leave and never come back. One of my favorites is the explanation of why the Sabbath is kept on the first day instead of the last day as the Father said. They have this wild and outrageous revelation which is nothing but an atrocity a deceptive perversion of the scriptures and is a down and out right lie! You can clearly see and read Yahushua did not ever go against the words of the Father YHWH. Because that is the will of the Father! Yahushua kept the Sabbath and the Feasts of YHWH. Yahushua is our sacrifice the Passover Lamb of YHWH. He is our teacher in truth, the kinsman redeemer of our souls. Let us not for get the meaning of Yahushua, YHWH is salvation. I need not remind you we are to become as He is, sons of YHWH. This is the real reason for the gift of His Spirit, the gift of life in us. So we can become sons of YHWH!

He was in the world, and the world was made by Him and the world knew Him not. 11 He came unto His own and His own received Him not. 12 But as many as received Him, to them gave He the power to become sons of YHWH, to them that believe on His name. 13 Which were born, not of blood, nor the will of the flesh, nor of the will of man, but the will of YHWH. (John 1:10-13)

Except a man be born again he cannot see the kingdom of YHWH. (John 3:3)

That means to be born from above, by the power of the spirit of Yahushua. The fact is, there is only one name of salvation for us in this day and time, Yahushua the Messiah.

20 Which he wrought in Messiah, when he raised him from the dead, and set him at his own right hand in the heavenly places, [21] Far above all principality, and power, and might, and dominion, and every name that is named, not only in this world, but also in that which is to come: [22] And hath put all things under his feet, and gave him to be the head over all things to the assembly, [23] Which is his body, the fulness of him that filleth all in all. (Eph 1:20-23)

When the apostle wrote this letter, or epistle to the Ephesians his descriptive, observation of Messiah was very large, so they would know the awesomeness of Yahushua's power and authority then and forever.

Yahushua came to them saying all authority and power in heaven and on earth has been given over to me. (Mat 28:18)

Then He spoke the way of salvation – so ye must be baptized and adhear to the commandments of the Father YHWH, which is our duty to him. The verse 23 in Eph 1, also says Yahushua is the one who (filleth all in all) this means He being our advocate our intercessor and Elohim He (answers or fulfills) all the prayers of the saints.

10 Be it known unto you all, and to all the people of Israel, that by the name of Yahushua of Nazareth, whom ye crucified, whom Elohim raised from the dead, even by him doth this man stand here before you whole. 11 This is the stone which was set at naught of you builders, which is become the head of the corner. 12 neither is there salvation in any other: for there is none other name under heaven given among men, whereby we must be saved. (Act 4:10-12)

I see it says name not names, singular not plural. It is a fact He only had the name Yahushua, if you would have called Him Jesus back then He would have not answered you. Remember the term replacement theology, this is why there are so many discrepancies in this days theology and understanding of the scriptures. Many people have handled the word and added even changed it to attain their own agenda, or their own belief. When you share with some one who is a believer on the name of Jesus and you say to them the real name of the Messiah is Yahushua, he or she will most likely say my bible says his name is Jesus, and that is all I need to know. But remember it is a changing of the scriptures! Even if it is a name change, it is still wrong! Those who are conscious of this fact realize the importance of His real name. This is what happened, they took the scriptures made and written by YHWH, with the original names and changed them. How could the Roman Catholics present the scriptures to the Roman people with Hebrew or Jewish names? They had to make them (un) Jewish. So the only way was to translate every name, make the scriptures look more like their language. Remember Constantine made Roman Catholicism the world wide religion. This was based on the use and reading of the scriptures written by the real holy men of YHWH's choosing. You see this fact of them making their own way, is a deception to those who follow. Also remember Eve was deceived by the changing of words when she listened to the serpent. I had many people say Oh He knows who I'm talking to, He knows my heart, and if that was so, why are you still calling Him by a wrong name. He told me His name Yahushua! It was not a deception, as many may think. But because of mans doctrine it took a while to find the truth of His real name. Many times people hear things in their spirit telling them, that which the ministers are saying or doing is wrong. But because they have always done it that way they do not even question the man but count what they heard in their spirit as a deception, how easy it is to disregard what we hear, when it shows us our wrong. We all are under obligated to search out the real way the truth, not disregard what we do not fully know, just because they do not do it that way. I also found out many people completely believe everything ministers and their wives say, even when it contradicts the truth. In this day and age there are many ministers gone a stray, I have even had ministers straight faced lie to others about me, even when they did not know me. They do it just to discredit me in the eyes of those who I have witnessed to. My point being, they are human and will do what it takes to accomplish their own agenda or achieve monetary gain. The proof is in the pudding so to speak, down through the ages there has been many that used the pulpit to achieve their goals. Many become ministers for prestige, money, power, rarely are they questioned, no matter what they say people take it as the truth, just because they are ministers. They know who they are and know the consequences of lying! That is the reason there are many wolves in sheep's clothing. So many are deceivers false teachers and have found out they can make a living off the masses and not have to do much. This is why we are to seek the truth and look beyond the pulpit of man and seek Him in the heavens, He who is the (Aleph and the Taw) the creator. Because the truth is we will be held accountable for ourselves, regardless what the preacher said.

My people are destroyed for lack of knowledge: because you have rejected knowledge, I will also reject thee, that thou shall be not priest to me: seeing thou has forgotten the law of thy Elohim, I will also forget thy children. (Hose 4:6)

Many will say I have not rejected knowledge! But you have, if you are following the Messiah Yahushua and you are not doing the will of the Father, or following as His word says we are to follow. I have heard many Christian ministers say from the pulpit, the Old Testament no longer applies to us! We are in the new Covenant, in this time. But on the contrary we are to become obedient to the Fathers will, and so the Torah, the Old Testament does apply to all of us who believe and follow the Messiah Yahushua. If anyone is the leader of a church or ministry and they are doing against scripture, and you do the same. That does not excuse you, it only means your blood will be on his hands when you perish. We will all be held accountable for our selves and what we have done. Those ministers will be held accountable to a higher degree of accountability than the average believer because they make their living off the word, as leaders of their own ministry. We are to be obedient to the heads and leaders of the nation we are apart of.

Be subject to every ordinance of man because of the Master Yahushua, whether to the King as supreme, 14. Or to governors, as to those who are sent by him for punishment of evil doers, and a praise for those who do good. 15 For so is the will of Elohim, that with well doing ye may put to silence the ignorance of foolish men: (1 Pet 2:13-15)

When we seek the truth in the scriptures and find it, it is our obligation to become obedient to the truth we learn, that is why it's in there, for our learning. YHWH already knows His word, He did not have it written so He would not forget but so we would learn and not forget. This also means when we search out a matter and learn of it we are to apply it in our lives the best we can, it is not our choice to pick and choose whether we like that rule or not, if it's in the rule book it can apply. It is a blatant disregard of the words in the scripture, that has caused the breakdown of real truth, concerning the scriptures. Because of the root of Christianity the understanding has been flawed by deception. The beginning of all Christianity is from Roman Catholicism! That is based on Romanism, paganism, Judaism with the belief in a Christ. It is no wonder they say all ways lead to heaven. The roman worship goes back to sexual misconduct and fornications, orgies, ect. Paganism was witch craft sorcery and all kinds of human sacrifices and blood rituals. Catholic churches mimic the Levitical priestly duties, and offerings, without sacrifice. Then worship of the woman Mary! and where is that in scripture? And praying to dead people, and relatives? Come on! None of that is scriptural at all. See that is the beginning of the tree Christianity, they had taken witch craft, worship of jove,

Jupiter, and zues and incorporated it into the way of what they called religion. None of which are biblical at all?

Have no other Elohim before me, make no likeness of any thing in the heavens above, or on the earth beneath, nor in the water under the earth. Do not bow down to them or serve them. For I YHWH am a jealous El visiting the iniquities of three to four generations of them who hate me. (Ex 20:3-5)

Some might think "Why is he knocking Christianity"? I am not! This is for your information, truth, to help you see what you have not been taught by the ministers of your congregations. It is vital truth, that many do not see, vital to your eternal life. Have you ever realized why the scriptures tell us to study to show our selves approved unto YHWH workman that need not be ashamed of rightly dividing the word of truth? So we will not be cast out into outer darkness, and so we walk into His real ways. Many places in scripture we are warned to learn, to do, to walk and become as Messiah. This being His purpose for our repentance and changing of heart. But what about those who partake of the gift of life in Messiah and do not become like Messiah or do not study regularly, and do not learn? What happens when they walk into the kingdom of YHWH as the promise of His word says.

[1] When he was come down from the mountain, great multitudes followed him. [2] And, behold, there came a leper and worshipped him, saying, Master, if thou wilt, thou canst

make me clean. 3 And Yahushua put forth his hand, and touched him, saying, I will; be thou clean. And immediately his leprosy was cleansed. 4 And Yahushua saith unto him, See thou tell no man; but go thy way, shew thyself to the priest, and offer the gift that Mosheh commanded, for a testimony unto them. 5 And when Yahushua was entered into Capernaum, there came unto him a centurion, beseeching him, 6 And saying, Master, my servant lieth at home sick of the palsy, grievously tormented. 7 And Yahushua saith unto him, I will come and heal him. 8 The centurion answered and said, Master, I am not worthy that thou shouldest come under my roof: but speak the word only, and my servant shall be healed. 9 For I am a man under authority, having soldiers under me: and I say to this man, Go, and he goeth; and to another, Come, and he cometh; and to my servant, Do this, and he doeth it. 10 When Yahushua heard it, he marveled, and said to them that followed, Verily I say unto you, I have not found so great faith, no, not in Israel. 11 And I say unto you, That many shall come from the east and west, and shall sit down with Abraham, and Isaac, and Jacob, in the kingdom of heaven. 12 But the children of the kingdom shall be cast out into outer darkness: there shall be weeping and gnashing of teeth. 13 And Yahushua said unto the centurion, Go thy way; and as thou hast believed, so be it done unto thee. And his servant was healed in the selfsame hour. (Mathew 8:1-13)

This is a reminder to show us we are at risk of being cast out into outer darkness should we become to complacent in faith and lacking in our understanding. Notice how Messiah connected the faith of the centurion with the belief of the Israeli people.

Verily I say unto you, I have not found so great faith, no, not in Israel. (Verse 10) Think who is Yahushua referring to?

[26] For ye are all the children of YHWH by faith in Messiah Yahushua. [27] For as many of you as have been baptized into Messiah Yahushua have put on Yahushua. [28] There is neither Jew nor Greek, there is neither bond nor free, there is neither male nor female: for ye are all one in Messiah Yahushua. [29] And if ye be Messiah's, then are ye Abraham's seed, and heirs according to the promise. (Gal 3:26-29)

Now who do you think Yahushua is referring to the Israeli people? Or all who are in the belief of Messiah? Remember Faith come by hearing and learning His words. The children are those who do not mature in to adult sons, as we are given the gift of life we are also to become mature. We all will go to sit down with Abraham, Yitshaq, and Ya'aqob in the kingdom of heaven. He was talking of those without faith and knowledge of Him and kingdom ways. He was talking of faith and total belief in Messiah, also known as kingdom ways. The only way to be in the kingdom is by belief in YHWH and His Yahushua, Then being born again and of water (John 3:3-5) which means the kingdom in all who follow and believe on Messiah, by the gift of life in us. Children are those who play in the play ground and never grow up! The Greek word huios means sons, children, beloved son, son of man. The translation of the word is children because of maturity and growth in Messiah, we all must become complete in Messiah. This also refers to those whom are of the old covenant after Yahushua paid the price for our wrongs, whom did not become sons according to the scriptures written in the book of John 3:3-5, search (Psalm 82:6-7) To be cast out into outer darkness is to be removed from life, complete and total separation from YHWH. This is why we must learn the ways of YHWH! Because many have rejected the truth, they have been desensitized and changed, from faith full to desiring more for the wrong reasons. Our goals and desire should be to become like Messiah Yahushua, and that only comes by the faith and knowledge of Him. By putting His word first in our thoughts, how many people really do that? How about you do you think what will Yahushua think. Or do you do things then think about the word? Look at your job if you have one, think how you do things day in day out. Many of those things you do become second nature to you, and you do them with out even thinking of your action. This is an automatic reaction to our life, and survival, what about when we die and our survival depends on what we think and know of Messiah Yahushua and YHWH the Father? Believe it or not our very existence will depend on it! YHWH knows our every thought and intent, we will not be able to hide even our deepest hidden secrets from Him. YHWH will know if we are kingdom minded or have selfish ambitions. Let's put it this way are you kingdom minded? Only the like mind of Messiah Yahushua in you will prove to be a delight to the Most High YHWH.

[1] Forasmuch then as Messiah hath suffered for us in the flesh, arm yourselves likewise with the same mind: for he that hath suffered in the flesh hath ceased from sin; [2] That he no longer should live the rest of his time in the flesh to the lusts of men, but to the will of YHWH. (1Pet 4:1-2)

We that are kingdom minded are to have a mind like Yahushua, with a desire to do the fathers will. That truly only comes by learning of Him and being like Him heart mind and soul. In the big picture, we are all going to be spiritual beings in the eternal. Thus we are to become sons like Him, heirs of (Salvation) in the true and original spirit of Messiah. The other spirit, the false Messiah spirit, the one that does not teach the Fathers will but mans ways, will not do! Because that spirit is against the true Messiah Yahushua! Because it is against the son Yahushua, that spirit is also against the Father YHWH who sent Him, all in that spirit will not live eternal but perish. The proof is in the actions of what is called the anti- messiah spirit, it is another spirit spoken of by the apostles. That spirit leads to death and not life, because it does not lead the persons to Yahushua but away from Him. One reason is replacement theology! Replacement theology is when you take the scriptures of Yahweh and incorporate them with another belief. Then what about unity in the spirit, does that exist in Christendom? Is it a myth in the world wide religion, called Christianity? What does the term truly cover over all, Catholicism is the base root of all Christianity and in fact is the beginning of the Christian tree. When you ask a catholic if they are a Christian they say no I'm catholic! But in all reality Christianity is of the catholic faith, because the root is from the catholic belief. Christianity is a continuation of Roman Catholicism, in it's newer form. This is why I say where is the unity? What is unity but all like believers in the same like mind and (belief!!!) hence the reason for that question.

This people draweth nigh unto me with their mouth, and honoureth me with their lips; but their heart is far from me. 9 But in vain they do worship me, teaching for doctrines the commandments of men. 10 And he called the multitude, and said unto them, Hear, and understand, 11 Not that which goeth into the mouth defileth a man; but that which cometh out of the mouth, this defileth a man.12 Then came his disciples, and said unto him, Knowest thou that the Pharisees were offended, after they heard this saying? 13 But he answered and said, every plant, which my heavenly Father hath not planted, shall be rooted up. (Mat 15:8-13)

We can see there are many different denominations of belief that are called Christian, each having different doctrinal beliefs. Yet they are calling themselves Christians! Many of the leaders are teaching their own denominational doctrine that differs from other Christian groups. In this day and age we are seeing what the apostle's wrote of.

[1] I charge thee therefore before YHWH, and the Master Yahushua the Messiah, who shall judge the quick and the dead at his appearing and his kingdom; [2] Preach the word; be instant in season, out of season; reprove, rebuke, exhort with all longsuffering and doctrine. [3] For the time will come when they will not endure sound doctrine; but after their own lusts shall they heap to themselves teachers, having itching ears; [4] And they shall turn away their ears from the truth, and shall be turned unto fables. (2Tim 4:1-4)

This has already come to pass for many generations. The religious leaders of Christianity seem to be more about the worldly things, than the spiritual, their focus seems to be more monetary, all about filling the church pews and adding on to the place they work at. Most preach what the people want to hear instead of what needs to be preached, that is the meaning of teachers with itching ears. The reason there are so many beliefs in the ranks of Christianity is the spirit that leads them, each one has a different spirit that guides them. They are different spirits! If unity was attainable in Christianity there would only be one doctrine, one belief, one way of salvation in Messiah and all would be in the same mind set. That is why the will of the Father YHWH is so important because when you do His will there is complete unity in truth and Spirit. The doctrine is the same, the way is the same, the Messiah Yahushua teaches all the same doctrine to His people by His Spirit. It really is a no brainier, if you do as the scriptures say then you will be doing correctly as Messiah Yahushua did. (He did the will of the Father) as we are called to do, just like He did, by walking as He walked, we are to follow in His steps! Yahushua spoke clearly to all of those learning of Him in the scriptures. Many have dismissed His still voice thinking it was a deceiving spirit because of doctrinal belief, clearly there is only one way not many. One reason so many say it is a matter of interpretation concerning the scriptures, is spiritual sight. Then total disregard for the true way, of the Father in heaven. This is why so many different ways, different spirits leading their sight.

18 We know that whosoever is born of Elohim sinneth
not; but he that is begotten of YHWH keepeth himself,
and that wicked one toucheth him not. 19 And we know
that we are of YHWH, and the whole world lieth in
wickedness. 20 And we know that the Son of YHWH is
come, and hath given us an understanding, that we may
know him that is true, and we are in him that is true, even
in his Son Yahushua ha Mashiyach. This is the true Elohim,
and eternal life. 21 Little children, keep yourselves from
idols. Amen. (1John 5:18-21)

This is the true sight of YHWH Yahushua ha Mashiyach, He is the way the truth and the life! None other is able to show anyone the true sight but Him as it clearly is the only name of salvation for all man kind. YHWH's beloved Son! The one we are to be fashioned after, the one we are to be like He is our savior our spiritual likeness.

1 Behold, what manner of love the Father hath bestowed upon us, that we should be called the sons of Elohim: therefore the world knoweth us not, because it knew him
not. 2 Beloved, now are we the sons of YHWH, and it doth not yet appear what we shall be: but we know that, when he shall appear, we shall be like him; for we shall see him as he is. (1John 3:1-2)

Regardless of anyone's opinion there is only one beloved son one spirit of life eternal. After that day when Yahushua ascended up into the heavens to be with the Father YHWH we all had to become sons or perish. The renewed covenant with which His blood was the payment for us all, that gave Him that right to be the King of Kings and our Salvation, in YHWH. He did what Adam was not able to achieve.

13 For until the law sin was in the world: but sin is not imputed when there is no law.

14 Nevertheless death reigned from Adam to Moses, even over them that had not sinned after the similitude of Adam's transgression, who is the figure of him that was to come. (Romans 5:13-14)

You can see Adam was put into death, spiritual death because of the transgression of Eve she ate of the tree then gave to Adam and he ate, but not by choice, because it was automatic they were one in spirit. The tree of knowledge of good and evil was the tree of deception, from that day on man could only enter in if he had overcome the evil works of the flesh. Remember what YHWH said (man has become like use to know good and evil)

[22] And YHWH said, Behold, the man is become as one
of us, to know good and evil: and now, lest he put forth his
hand, and take also of the tree of life, and eat, and live for
ever: [23] There- fore YHWH sent him forth from the garden
of Eden, to till the ground from whence he was taken. [24] So
he drove out the man; and he placed at the east of the garden
of Eden Cherubims, and a flaming sword which turned
every way, to keep the way of the tree of life. (Gen 3:22-24)

The fact is nothing is impossible to YHWH He is able to do anything. As it does seem in scripture YHWH loves His people and knows what they go through, because deception is a power over mankind by the lust of the flesh. And we must remember YHWH temps no man. Temptation is a tool of familiar spirits, and evil wickedness. That is why the scriptures tell us to overcome the works of the flesh, so that evil will have no power over you. It is YHWH's desire that we all have authority over the spirit of sin.

As he told Cain before he slew his brother Able. But because of sin the created is at enmity with the creator, the man cannot have fellowship with YHWH in the spirit of death. Only when man turns to YHWH in true repentance and a need to change.

6 And YHWH said unto Cain, Why art thou wroth?
and why is thy countenance fallen?
7 If thou doest well, shalt thou not be accepted ? and if
thou doest not well, sin lieth at the door. And unto thee
shall be his desire, and thou shalt rule over him. Gen 4:6-7

That is why all mankind is born into death from the start of life on this earth, without choice, but given free will to seek the creator and His ways, to become one of His and set free indeed. Now many are born into families that are not believers or are against YHWH that is a generational curse. That curse can last as long as three to four generations.

3 Thou shalt have no other elohim before me. 4 Thou shalt
not make unto thee any graven image, or any likeness of any
thing that is in heaven above, or that is in the earth beneath, or
that is in the water under the earth: 5 Thou shalt not bow down
thyself to them, nor serve them: for I YHWH thy Elohim
am a jealous El, visiting the iniquity of the fathers upon the
children unto the third and fourth generation of them that
hate me; 6 And shewing mercy unto thousands of them that
love me, and keep my commandments. (Exodus 20:3-6)

This applies to every living person on the earth, either you are or are not, there is no in between, or middle ground there. Those who believe and seek him are under the true mercies of YHWH, those who do not are under the law or Torah like it or not. The choice is not your own, but is the fundamental principal of all mankind, life or death, right or wrong, good or evil. That is the basic reason for free will, we all who are going to be in the (New Yerusalem) will be there by choice not force. YHWH forces no man into heaven or to be His son! We all who are His love Him and are heirs of Salvation because of His wonderful working in our lives. He had also showed us His immense love, you see every single wrong or false religion is lead by the deceiver, what better way to assure the end of man than letting them think they are correct, in all their wrong ways and false god. YHWH corrects and chastens His sons, false gods let them stay lawless and in wrong ways and thinking. Remember satan is a copy cat who has made the other or false Messiah to deceive the masses as scripture has said. The false messiah does not direct people to the real true way of YHWH. But an open door to easy, warm fuzzy, feel goods, that is a deception that causes strong delusion, and keeps people from seeing real truth, because of feelings and religious liberality. Because there are ways that seem right to man but are deceptive practices that lead to spiritual death.

8 And then shall the lawless one be revealed whom
the Master shall consume with the spirit of his mouth,
and shall destroy with the brightness of his coming: 9
Even him, whose coming is after the working of Satan
with all power and signs and lying wonders, 10 And with
all deceivableness of unrighteousness in them that perish;
because they received not the love of the truth, that they
might be saved. 11 And for this cause Elohim shall send
them strong delusion, that they should believe a lie: 12 That

they all might be damned who believed not the truth, but had pleasure in unrighteousness. (2Thes 2:8-12)

Proof the anti Messiah spirit was already at work when the first twelve apostles were walking the earth, because they all warned us through the scriptures. It was here already! And since then that spirit was able to cover the earth, perpetrating false signs and wonders, to many people under the delusion. Every person under that delusion some where along the time line of their life rejected the real truth for the man made truth, just because it was not the normal way. Here is a way to look at it, a short explanation- a family that has familiar spirits and practices witch craft, teaches their children after them and so on. Is that the way of life? NO! but to them it is because that is what they are taught to do, and believe it or not they even think they will have salvation, many even think they are chosen of Elohim to do evil against the righteous. All who know the scriptures realize there deception but they do not. Well the false Messiah is the same way, that spirit teaches them parts of the way in the scriptures. Now a days there are so many religions doing things that is against the scriptures, even those who are taught by them do against His word. Why? Deception! Many of the people who go to those religious places do not even question the things being done. Roman Catholicism is a perfect example of unscriptural ways, and false worship, no where in the scriptures does it say all ways lead to heaven. Nor does it say anything about praying to Mary, or dead people, or past ministers, or apostles, or priests. But on the contrary it says other wise! Because any thing or any one you pray to is your spiritual leader, your Elohim or your god.

Yahushua said: 13 ask anything in my name and it will be done, I will do it that the Father be glorified in the Son, 14 ask anything I will do it! (John 14:13-14)

YHWH said: 3 Have no other Elohim before Me. [4] Thou shalt not make unto thee any graven image, or any likeness of any thing that is in heaven above, or that is in the earth beneath, or that is in the water under the earth: [5] Do not bow down thyself to them, nor serve them: for I YHWH am a jealous El, visiting the iniquity of the fathers upon the children unto the third and fourth generation of them that hate me; (Ex 20:3-5)

[15] Take ye therefore good heed unto yourselves; for ye saw no manner of similitude on the day that YHWH spake unto you in Horeb out of the midst of the fire: [16] Lest ye corrupt yourselves, and make you a graven image, the similitude of any figure, the likeness of male or female, [17] The likeness of any beast that is on the earth, the likeness of any winged fowl that flieth in the air, [18] The likeness of any thing that creepeth on the ground, the likeness of any fish that is in the waters beneath the earth: [19] And lest thou lift up thine eyes unto heaven, and when thou seest the sun, and the moon, and the stars, even all the host of heaven, shouldest be driven to worship them, and serve them,

which YHWH thy Elohim hath divided unto all nations under the whole heaven. (Deu 4:15-19)

It is very clear YHWH did not want any one of His people to worship anything other than Him. If you pray to any one or thing that is a form of worship, so if you keep His Scriptures you are following Him, that is worship, and worship to any other is Idolatry! See how serious that was to the Creator of all!

[2] If there be found among you, within any of thy gates which YHWH thy Elohim giveth thee, man or woman, that hath wrought wickedness in the sight of YHWH thy Elohim, in transgressing his covenant, [3] And hath gone and served other gods, and worshipped them, either the sun, or moon, or any of the host of heaven, which I have not commanded; [4] And it be told thee, and thou hast heard of it, and enquired diligently, and, behold, it be true, and the thing certain, that such abomination is wrought in Israel: [5] Then shalt thou bring forth that man or that woman, which have committed that wicked thing, unto thy gates, even that man or that woman, and shalt stone them with stones, till they die. (Deu 17:2-5)

The reason YHWH said those things to his people, He did not want them to do as the heathen did, who worshipped sun and stars, rocks, wood, carved images and such. He did not want to be known as their gods or their leader because he hated their practices and their ways. That is why He made such a steep penalty, idolatry! Is death.

When Israel was under the complete direction of YHWH He had every thing covered that could be imagined. If you read the story of king David and his son (Shalomoh / Salomon), you will see they were blessed until the kings fell into bad ways or idolatry! It was not until then they were given over to other nations because of the wrong ways. Shalomoh committed idolatry and lost favor from YHWH! You can see the pattern of good and blessings then evil and captivity, through out the entire history of the scriptures. The final clincher was when they gave their infant children over to molech, as it is written:

[21] And thou shalt not let any of thy seed pass through the fire to Molech neither shalt thou profane the name of thy Elohim: I am YHWH. (Lev 18:21) also [1] And YHWH spake unto Mosheh, saying, [2] Again, thou shalt say to the children of Israel, Whosoever he be of the children of Israel, or of the strangers that sojourn in Israel, that giveth any of his seed unto Molech; he shall surely be put to death: the people of the land shall stone him with stones. [3] And I will set my face against that man, and will cut him off from among his people; because he hath given of his seed unto Molech, to defile my sanctuary, and to profane my holy name. [4] And if the people of the land do any ways hide their eyes from the man, when he giveth of his seed unto Molech, and kill him not: [5] Then I will set my face against that man, and against his family, and will cut him off, and all that go a whoring after him, to commit whoredom with Molech,

from among their people. [6] And the soul that turneth after such as have familiar spirits, and after wizards, to go a whoring after them, I will even set my face against that soul, and will cut him off from among his people. (Lev 20:1-6)

YHWH said, do not do the things those other nations did to their gods. But they did as He said not to!

[26] Then came the word of YHWH unto Jeremiah, saying, [27] Behold, I am YHWH, the Elohim of all flesh: is there any thing too hard for me? [28] Therefore thus saith YHWH; Behold, I will give this city into the hand of the Chaldeans, and into the hand of Nebuchadrezzar king of Babylon, and he shall take it: [29] And the Chaldeans, that fight against this city, shall come and set fire on this city, and burn it with the houses, upon whose roofs they have offered incense unto Baal, and poured out drink offerings unto other els, to provoke me to anger. [30] For the children of Israel and the children of Judah have only done evil before me from their youth: for the children of Israel have only provoked me to anger with the work of their hands, saith YHWH. [31] For this city hath been to me as a provocation of mine anger and of my fury from the day that they built it even unto this day; that I should remove it from before my face, [32] Because of all the evil of the children of Israel and of the children of Judah, which they have done to provoke me to anger, they, their kings, their princes, their priests, and their prophets, and the men of Judah, and the inhabitants of Jerusalem. [33] And they have turned unto me the back and not the face:

though I taught them, rising up early and teaching them, yet they have not hearkened to receive instruction. [34] But they set their abominations in the house, which is called by my name, to defile it. [35] And they built the high places of Baal, which are in the valley of the son of Hinnom, to cause their sons and their daughters to pass through the fire unto Molech; which I commanded them not, neither came it into my mind, that they should do this abomination, to cause Judah to sin. [36] And now therefore thus saith YHWH thee Elohim of Yisra'el, concerning this city, whereof ye say, It shall be delivered into the hand of the king of Babylon by the sword, and by the famine, and by the pestilence; (Jer 32:26-36)

Every time a righteous King followed the word of YHWH, they were at peace and had much fruitfulness and victory in all the dealing with every other nation and peoples. That is the key, to a blessed nation, if the leader of the nation is righteous and following YHWH whole hearted in spirit and in truth! That nation will be blessed by YHWH completely, HalleluYah! The fact of the matter Molech was the god of the Ammonites, and the Phoenicians, the deity to whom some of the Yisraelites sacrificed their infant children to. That was a last straw to YHWH when they did that, His wrath was kindled very strongly against them. He then turned them over to the Chaldeans, the Chaldeans were people of wizardry and witch craft, they had many spiritual ways, one of was star gazing and reading the heavens.

[10] There shall not be found among you any one that
maketh his son or his daughter to pass through the fire, or
that useth divination, or an observer of times, or an enchanter,
or a witch, [11] Or a charmer, or a consulter with familiar
spirits, or a wizard, or a necromancer. [12] For all that do these
things are an abomination unto YHWH thy Elohim: and
because of these abominations YHWH thy Elohim doth
drive them out from before thee. (Deu 18:10-12)

The Chaldeans were to them a people that showed them the error of their ways, by the example of their way of life. The Chaldeans were people of witch craft, sorcery, star gazing and followers of the black arts.

("CHALDAEANS" are a priest caste, with a peculiar tongue and learning, skilled in divination. They were also worshipers of jupiter, zeus, neptune and did much enchantments- Source- Dictionary.com)

[30] For the children of Israel and the children of Judah
have only done evil before me from their youth: for the
children of Israel have only provoked me to anger with the
work of their hands, saith YHWH. [31] For this city hath been
to me *as* a provocation of mine anger and of my fury from
the day that they built it even unto this day; that I should
remove it from before my face,[32] Because of all the evil of
the children of Israel and of the children of Judah, which
they have done to provoke me to anger, they, their kings,
their princes, their priests, and their prophets, and the men
of Judah, and the inhabitants of Jerusalem. (Jer 32:30-32)

History has repeated itself over and over, after that the children of Yisra'el had been in captivity many generations and by many different nations, one being the Romans! Of which had kept the Israeli people in captivity almost 600 years. During the time of Messiah's ministry and life the Romans ruled over Israel, and even during Messiah's crucifixion, remember the religious Jewish leaders had to get permission and falsify Messiah's crimes so it would become His end. Little did they know He would be the ruler over the heavens and earth. Yahushua ha Mashiyach who's throne will never end!

Many people do not know Constantine was riding both sides of the fence so to speak, he was a cult leader as he also was a Roman dictator. Which means he practiced witch craft and other divinations. He was also the leader that proclaimed Roman Catholicism as the world wide religion. Roman Catholicism was made up of romanism, paganism, and ritualism, mimicking the Levitical priest hood. They called themselves Vickers of Christ, and considered themselves Messiah's replacement on earth. That was the beginning of (Christianity) and the almost end of the Jewish faith. Many Hebrew people snuck out of Yisra'el in the night watch to escape the Roman persecution. The Yisra'eli people had no protection from them or their idiotic laws. They were forced to ware stars on their clothing to make others aware they were Jewish. Those that stayed were forced to take full part in the Roman Catholic (papacy / religion) and had to renounce their previous belief, publicly. The facts concerning the religious crusades, they were killing and destroying any one that had the scriptural knowledge of truth and believed on the Messiah, but not according to the Catholic papacy. They did not seek out witches to burn but true believers in Messiah. The fact is witch craft was incorporated into their faith, and still is in small increments. Like man worship, candle lighting, praying to dead relatives, all these are like (demonic cult practices). These are practices of those with familiar spirits, witches and necromancers. I had found out in my studies and travels the majority of the people in the world do not believe witches or wizards even exist. I really believe many have become desensitized, and have lost their moralistic values with constant thoughts of witch craft, magic, werewolves, vampirism, death, ect because television and its movie magic and television has even taught people to believe or think there is such a thing as a good witch. Calling them white witches, which are supposed to be doers of good and not evil, funny the scriptures do not say that.

[18] Thou shalt not suffer a witch to live. (Ex 22:18)

Now that does not say good witch because there is no such thing. If you know what a witch really is and does, you would never think them good at all. They are like vampires, they steal the precious life right out of a person. I even think that is a real revelation of where the story of vampirism came from because they are very much alike. You see witches lack real spirit, they are lead by a familiar spirit, a spirit of death and the spirit in them is always leading them to a spirit that has the life force still in tacked. Some say they have jezebel spirits which could be a possibility. Either way they are very ruthless and have no moral limitations, and steal from any one that is available young and old. Remember the story of Hansel and Gretel that was based on truth, witches steal from children even their own because they are easy prey. Witches are the walking dead, like zombies outside there are no signs of death. Given the chance they will steal your little child's gift of life in a heart beat. How did witches come to be? The tree of knowledge of good and evil! From that day on man was in death until cleansed by the Spirit of life, YHWH and Yahushua the Messiah. Woman is to be under her husbands covering, when she is a little girl she is under her fathers covering and the deity of her father, regardless of his belief of life or death. The same is for the son he is under his fathers' deity and cover, the man is to be the spiritual leader of his house. YHWH set the order which is by His design, like it or not this is His order and for His purpose His reason not mans.

[3] But I would have you know, that the head of every man is Messiah; and the head of the woman is the man; and the head of Messiah, YHWH. (1Cor 11:3)

[11] Nevertheless neither is the man without the woman,
neither the woman without the man, in the YHWH. [12] For
as the woman is of the man, even so is the man also by the woman; but all things of Elohim.(1Cor 11:11-12)

In short YHWH does not see the man without the woman or the woman without the man! They are one flesh independently one spirit, one together as heirs of salvation or unto death.

1 Likewise, ye wives, be in subjection to your own
husbands; that, if any obey not the word, they also may
without the word be won by the conversation of the wives;
2 While they behold your chaste conversation coupled with
fear. 3 Whose adorning let it not be that outward adorning
of plaiting the hair, and of wearing of gold, or of putting
on of apparel; 4 But let it be the hidden man of the heart,
in that which is not corruptible, even the ornament of a
meek and quiet spirit, which is in the sight of YHWH
of great price. 5 For after this manner in the old time
the holy women also, who trusted in YHWH, adorned
themselves, being in subjection unto their own husbands: 6
Even as Sara obeyed Abraham, calling him master: whose
daughters ye are, as long as ye do well, and are not afraid
with any amazement. 7 Likewise, ye husbands, dwell with
them according to knowledge, giving honour unto the wife,
as unto the weaker vessel, and as being heirs together of the
grace of life; that your prayers be not hindered. (1Pet 3:1-7)

When a woman marries, her husband is her spiritual leader and his covering or deity is also then her deity, in life or death. If the woman is in the belief of life and he is in death then she steps back into darkness with her husband. And on the other note the man if he is a believer and she is in death when they come together there is then an open door of death to him, sin has entered in to the house. They being of one flesh share in the sins of their help mate. If either one of them commits adultery, they are doing witch craft because adultery is a part of witch craft. That is one reason YHWH does not like the mixing of the spirits among His people, theft. A woman makes herself a witch when she sleeps with men just to be joined into there spiritual life, or because of his gift of strength. Harlotry, promiscuity, being a whoremonger, and adultery are all death to the man or woman. They are an abomination to YHWH, it is witchcraft, also blatant disobedience to Him and His word. I will say this, ignorance is not an excuse, in this day and age everyone who reads the bible or walks in the earth has heard it is wrong to commit adultery. Although many choose to ignore that statement, in the world it has consequences that are not good, YHWH's word says it is death. Even now a days there are generations of witches and wizards each taught by their parents or parent. You see young girls make them selves witches, spiritual thieves, by sleeping around, that is witch craft and death to the female because it is also adultery. When a female joins with a man and she is a witch she does the act to steal from the man, his strength, his precious life. Young men become dead men by the same act, they become spiritually dead. Women are conduits because of the womb they house the joining of the spirits with their husband, this completes them together in marriage. Now he is in her and she is with him, together they are one spirit one flesh in the spiritual and the earthly. When the man is joined to his wife their hearts are one together, this makes his love toward her unique and increased. That is also saying if he is capable of love, some people are not. And she is also increased in love toward her husband. But when not married here is the consequence, spiritual blindness and death. The scriptures do not lie!

[24] To keep thee from the evil woman, from the flattery of the tongue of a strange woman. [25] Lust not after her beauty in thine heart; neither let her take thee with her eyelids. [26] For by means of a whorish woman a man is brought to a piece of bread: and the adulteress will hunt for the precious life. [27] Can a man take fire in his bosom, and his clothes not be burned? [28] Can one go upon hot coals, and his feet not be burned? [29] So he that goeth in to his neighbour's wife; whosoever toucheth her shall not be innocent. [30] Men do not despise a thief, if he steal to satisfy his soul when he is hungry; [31] But if he be found, he shall restore sevenfold; he shall give all the substance of his house. [32] But whoso committeth adultery with a woman lacketh understanding he that doeth it destroyeth his own soul. [33] A wound and dishonour shall he get; and his reproach shall not be wiped away. [34] For jealousy is the rage of a man: therefore he will not spare in the day of vengeance. [35] He will not regard any ransom; neither will he rest content, though thou givest many gifts. (Pro 6:24-35)

1 My son, attend unto my wisdom, and bow thine ear
to my understanding: 2 That thou mayest regard discretion,
and that thy lips may keep knowledge. 3 For the lips of a
strange woman drop as an honeycomb, and her mouth is
smoother than oil: 4 But her end is bitter as wormwood,
sharp as a two edged sword. 5 Her feet go down to death;
her steps take hold on hell. 6 Lest thou shouldest ponder
the path of life, her ways are moveable, that thou canst not
know them. 7 Hear me now therefore, O ye children, and
depart not from the words of my mouth. 8 Remove thy way
far from her, and come not nigh the door of her house: 9
Lest thou give thine honour unto others, and thy years unto
the cruel: 10 Lest strangers be filled with thy wealth and thy
labours be in the house of a stranger; 11 And thou mourn
at the last, when thy flesh and thy body are consumed,
12 And say, How have I hated instruction, and my heart
despised reproof; 13 And have not obeyed the voice of my
teachers, nor inclined mine ear to them that instructed me!
14 I was almost in all evil in the midst of the congregation
and assembly. 15 Drink waters out of thine own cistern, and
running waters out of thine own well. 16 Let thy fountains
be dispersed abroad, and rivers of waters in the streets. 17
Let them be only thine own, and not strangers' with thee.
18 Let thy fountain be blessed: and rejoice with the wife
of thy youth. 19 Let her be as the loving hind and pleasant
roe; let her breasts satisfy thee at all times; and be thou
ravished always with her love. 20 And why wilt thou, my

son, be ravished with a strange woman, and embrace the bosom of a stranger? [21] For the ways of man are before the eyes of YHWH, and he pondereth all his goings. [22] His own iniquities shall take the wicked himself, and he shall be holden with the cords of his sins [23] He shall die without instruction; and in the greatness of his folly he shall go astray. (Pro 5)

The consequence is very severe and hard to accept, to hard for many, and unknown to others. It is because man is to be the spiritual head, the leader of their marital union, this is why he has so much to lose. When a man and woman are together then become divorced they both are adulterers, but the woman becomes like that of a lost soul without her covering. Now this does not mean they cannot repent they can, but it must be in proper accordance with the word of YHWH. (You must get Messiah, Yahushua) in your heart and soul as (John 3:3) same as (Romans 10:9-10, & 11-13) Yahushua the Messiah is the only way to a clean slate, and the confession of our wrong.

[8] If we say that we have no sin, we deceive ourselves, and the truth is not in us. [9] If we confess our sins, he is faithful and just to forgive us our sins, and to cleanse us from all unrighteousness. (1John 1:8-9)

That is the only way to get ride of your sin, and when the time is right then ye must be baptized into the real true name of the Messiah Yahushua. It is very important to be baptized by a man already in the true name baptism of Yahushua. Because he is a witness, and Yahushua our Savior is a witness the Holy Spirit is a witness the Father YHWH and these three agree in one. In the earth man, to make him a complete spirit man in his Elohim with knowledge and revelations of His word and favor with the Father YHWH. Now it is a real chance of redemption, and a complete cleansing of your inner being. To repent means you must turn away from your wrongs and do not do them any more, and adultery is death so it is much better to be married than to burn. Yahushua also said if you look and think the act in your mind you have already committed the act of adultery. The mind is the battle field, 99% of the times when your mind gives in your body follows. That is why we are so prone to the temptations of the flesh, the lust of the flesh starts in the mind. That is why we must renew are minds with His words and not the unrighteous thoughts of lustful pleasures. The scriptures is the power over the works of the flesh and evil thoughts. Because His word has the power of His Spirit it breaks down the walls of our captivity and frees our mind from the bondage of the deadly thoughts. As we learn of the Master and His way we become more like Him and less of what we used to be. This is why we are to teach our children the truth about the joining of the souls, and the real reason we should not have multiple relationship out side the bond of the marriage. You see television and the movies glorifies sex and use it as a tool to sell their product. But in all reality they are selling you into death, and making all who watch, think it is ok to do those things, but it is not ok, because it is death. Sexual contact out side of the marriage, destroys your life, in any form, because it is adultery, and most often fornication. Because of fornication and adultery witch craft and wizardry is unseen in the eyes of their prey. Witches will sleep with anyone to join into that person's spiritual gift, so they can steal, plunder and destroy that person's life for their own increase. They make you think you are something to be desired then lure you into the act of intercourse but once you put your seed in them you are joined into there death, and your gift of life is then being jeopardized or possibly stolen from you. This is also a very important thing to know, many witches will steal from your little children, because they are easy prey. So be ware of strangers around your children, or who you let into their lives, and especially who you give authority over your children. That could make a lot of things happen in the lives of your children that need not be. Many people do not believe witches even exist but they do and there are more of them in this world than you would even realize. That is also the same of the wizards as well, they also prey upon others to steal the precious life or spiritual blessings. Because those that are witches give it to them, wizards go after the wives of men who are blessed or have much strength. The wizards use many methods the easiest is adultery, but they, the wizards and witches resort to many different methods, drug sorcery, date rape drugs.

None the less if or when they get another mans wife to have a adulteress relationship with them, they take all they can, kind of like extortion. Give to me or I will tell your husband! She is then in bondage, like a slave they will use her like a whore. Many men go through the same thing but in a different way. Either way it eventually destroys their marriage, which is satans goal toward all the marriages, because of the importance of marriage to YHWH the Father. He made marriage His perfect design for a reason! And so satan the evil one is trying to destroy YHWH's plan and reason for the marriages that are His. The righteous marriages are the most attacked union on this earth! A proper marriage is a holy union before YHWH, one man one woman in love and dedication to YHWH. The depths the force of darkness will go to, is what ever it takes. That is one motto of those who serve familiar spirits, what ever it takes, that has very bad implications and is a true, because they are usually sent by false gods of evil to destroy the righteous. Adultery is a form of witch craft, because they use the joining of the souls to destroy and steel from others unknowingly. Their whole goal is to take what you have and use it for themselves, as in (Proverbs 5) Many say no one can take anything from me, that is impossible! But I assure you, the scriptures tells us to be on guard lest we be naked.

15 Behold, I come as a thief. Blessed is he that watcheth, and keepeth his garments, lest he walk naked, and they see his shame. (Rev16:15)

That scripture has two fold meaning, as a person may become complacent, or lukewarm thinking they know all, even stagnant in the way of scripture knowledge through arrogance and pride. This also is a reminder that we can lose our blessing of salvation. We cannot ever think this gift of life has unconditional favor over all the continuing ways of sin.

He that overcometh, the same shall be clothed in white raiment; and I will not blot out his name out of the book of life, but I will confess his name before my Father, and before his angels. (Rev 3:5)

28 Let them be blotted out of the book of the living, and
not be written with the righteous. (Psalm 69:28)

In this day of modern technology and scientific advancement there is also a factor of drug sorcery, such as hypnotic and mind altering drugs, date rape drugs, sodium pentothal, and many other types of controlling drugs that make people puppets to another's will. And so to be naked is to be without the gift of life, the word keepeth means to guard your self and your precious life. Those who serve the forces of darkness or blatantly reject YHWH and the Son Yahushua are not going to have life eternal. But outer darkness is their end as the scriptures declare.

5 And he that sat upon the throne said, Behold, I make
all things new. And he said unto me, Write: for these words
are true and faithful. 6 And he said unto me, It is done. I am
Alpha and Omega, the beginning and the end. I will give

unto him that is athirst of the fountain of the water of life freely. [7] He that overcometh shall inherit all things and I will be his Elohim, and he shall be my son.[8] But the fearful, and unbelieving, and the abominable, and murderers, and whoremongers, and sorcerers, and idolaters, and all liars, shall have their part in the lake which burneth with fire and brimstone: which is the second death. (Rev 21:5-8)

[15] For without are dogs, and sorcerers, and whoremongers, and murderers, and idolaters, and whosoever loveth and maketh a lie. (Rev 22:15)

I had thought on this verse and realized many people say the term dogs, is a metaphor to show a person with an impure mind, as if YHWH had to make it clear about those who were not of the correct mind set. But regarding that, outside the gates of the heavenly home is outer darkness and a place of punishment not reward. Dogs is meant in a literal and figurative sense because the word in Strong's -

(kuon- of the Strong's G2965 pronounced ~ koo-ohn is literally the word for hound- dog) then we must look at the other meaning of dog –

(H3611- keleb, pronounced keh-leb means (to yelp, or else to attack; translates as "dog" 32 times. 1 dog. 1A dog (literal). 1B contempt or abasement, 1C of pagan sacrifice. 1D of male cult prostitute (fig).

When YHWH used the word dogs His intent was to show the state of a man's mind, the actions of man, and the terror of retribution or disgust. Because of mans idolatries, evils, and blatant disobedience, YHWH used the term dog or dogs to make all people realize the terror He would bring upon them because of their actions and ingratitude for His blessings on there lives. Many times it was said the dogs would eat their flesh and drink their blood. YHWH is using the term dog and dogs to show eating and devouring in the Torah. Then even in the new covenant scriptures there are references to dogs and dog eating or devouring, either way it was brought in to light to show punishment and disgust. A dog is an unclean animal, many cultures used them as warning instruments, and guard animals, and many also used them as food and pets. In many other countries dogs are considered scavengers and have no real purpose in society. To give or throw to the dogs, is to throw away, as useless, or to go to the dogs is to be ruined. But now think of it as punishment as YHWH said the dogs will tear and eat your flesh, drink and lick your blood, in the same time referring to without or outside the confines of the eternal city which is outer darkness total isolation away from the hope of life or Salvation, but a place of punishment. Because He already covered the abase man, the whoremonger which is male and female prostitutes and fornicators, then liars, murderers, sorcerers, idolaters. YHWH is able to do anything He desires and He has no limits at all, here in the temporal or in the eternal. You also must realize wizards make themselves the god of witches and those who know not any real truth, but deceptions from familiar spirits and such. Which I will add is the worst form of idolatry that man perpetrates, to make one's self another person's god! YHWH hates that and makes a real example out of those people here in the temporal and in the eternal.

1 And YHWH spake unto Moses, saying, 2 Again, thou shalt say to the children of Israel, Whosoever he be of the children of Israel, or of the strangers that sojourn in Israel, that giveth any of his seed unto Molech; he shall surely be put to death: the people of the land shall stone him with stones. 3 And I will set my face against that man, and will cut him off from among his people; because he hath given of his seed unto Molech, to defile my sanctuary, and to profane my holy name. 4 And if the people of the land do any ways hide their eyes from the man, when he giveth of his seed unto Molech, and kill him not: 5 Then I will set my face against that man, and against his family, and will cut him off, and all that go a whoring after him, to commit whoredom with Molech, from among their people. 6 And the soul that turneth after such as have familiar spirits, and after wizards, to go a whoring after them, I will even set my face against that soul, and will cut him off from among his people. (Lev 20:1-6)

See how serious YHWH took the act of idolatry, He made it a personal and important issue, because they profaned His Holy name and rejected Him over false elohim and men with familiar spirits. So I know YHWH has a sense of humor and vengeance so why will there not be dogs out side in outer darkness to bring all those self-proclaimed gods to a place of punishment and terror beyond the wildest dreams and thoughts of our finite minds. Because David said: if I make my bed in hell thou art there, he who dwells in the thick darkness! And YHWH will repay them to their face them that hate Him! YHWH has no limitations. (DEU 18:15-19)

None shall escape His wrath that hate him. Those who make any man other than Messiah Yahushua their Savior and Elohim, will perish without mercy, and before they are put into the lake of fire and brimstone the terror of YHWH will be upon them. That is the worst place to ever be, cut off from YHWH. Can a man or woman repent of such evil doings? Maybe, but it is only by the mercy of YHWH through the beloved Son Yahushua the Messiah.

[27] A man also or woman that hath a familiar spirit, or that is a wizard, shall surely be put to death: they shall stone them with stones: their blood shall be upon them. (Lev 20:27)

The thing many people do not realize is, this temporal place called earth, is the proving ground for us to become spiritual sons of YHWH. Because we are the ones replacing those who were cast out into outer darkness in chains of darkness until the great day, those angles that went against YHWH's rules and followed the dragon, satan. YHWH has made many fail safes, and tests for His people to be cleansed. Only He can know the true state of mans heart. If we think we will have it our way, think again, it will be His way and none other than His. Remember outer darkness is a place of punishment and a place of total exile away from the light of life. Just like the deeps of hell or sheol, for some reason many religious beliefs seem to think it does not exist or is not a place of punishment but a place to repent after they have made retribution. WRONG that is not the way it is, all these places are part of His fail safes, His rest is only for His people that are His and love Him, and do His will. The places called, (hell, sheol, hades,) outer darkness, death are all places of destruction not retribution or repentance none will be able to make it through those and live. When you are brought out of either of those places you will not have a straight thought in your being. Because the crazies is all you'll have, none can cope with the horrors that await them in those places.

[19] There was a certain rich man, which was clothed in
purple and fine linen, and fared sumptuously every day: [20]
And there was a certain beggar named Lazarus, which was
laid at his gate, full of sores, [21] And desiring to be fed with
the crumbs which fell from the rich man's table: moreover
the dogs came and licked his sores. [22] And it came to pass,
that the beggar died, and was carried by the angels into
Abraham's bosom: the rich man also died, and was buried;
[23] And in hell he lift up his eyes, being in torments, and
seeth Abraham afar off, and Lazarus in his bosom. [24] And
he cried and said, Father Abraham, have mercy on me, and
send Lazarus, that he may dip the tip of his finger in water,

and cool my tongue; for I am tormented in this flame. [25] But Abraham said, Son, remember that thou in thy lifetime receivedst thy good things, and likewise Lazarus evil things: but now he is comforted, and thou art tormented. [26] And beside all this, between us and you there is a great gulf fixed: so that they which would pass from hence to you cannot; neither can they pass to us, that would come from thence. [27] Then he said, I pray thee therefore, father, that thou wouldest send him to my father's house: [28] For I have five brethren; that he may testify unto them, lest they also come into this place of torment. [29] Abraham saith unto him, they have Moses and the prophets; let them hear them. [30] And he said, nay, father Abraham: but if one went unto them from the dead, they will repent. [31] And he said unto him, if they hear not Moses and the prophets, neither will they be persuaded, though one rose from the dead. (Luke 16:19-31).

What do you think torment really means? I do think if you would like more proof of hell it is in the scriptures.

The Greek word for hell is (geenna – pronounced gheh-en-enah, Strong's G1067) meaning- Hell is the place of the future punishment call "Gehenna" or "Gehenna of fire". This was originally the valley of Hinnom, south of Jerusalem, where the filth and dead animals of the city were cast out and burned; a fit symbol of the wicked and their future destruction. The Hebrew word is (Sheol – Strong's H7585) – 1 sheol, underworld, grave, hell, pit. 1A the underworld. 1B Sheol—the OT designation for the abode of the dead. *1B1* place of no return. *1B2* without praise of Elohim. Wicked sent there for punishment. 1B4 righteous not abandoned to it. 1B5 of the place of exile (fig). of extreme degradation in sin.

Make no mistake hell is a place of torment and destruction. So those who teach hell is just a repenting place are misleading all who believe and listen to them. Remember the price for wrong doing must be appeased there is no way out of the cost, the price is, no life everlasting. There is no way to cheat your maker, these are some of His fail safes that are automatic, just like gravity. The only way for that not to happen to you is repent call upon Yahushua the Messiah and confess all the wrong doings in your life so you can become cleansed.

9 If we confess our sins, he is faithful and just to forgive us our sins, and to cleanse us from all unrighteousness. (1John 1:9)

Yohanan or John the Baptist called the people to repentance, because he was the one making straight the road to Yahushua, as was written in the prophets.

1 In those days came John the Baptist, preaching in the wilderness of Judaea,

2 And saying, Repent ye: for the kingdom of heaven is
at hand. 3 For this is he that was spoken of by the prophet
Esaias, saying, The voice of one crying in the wilderness,
Prepare ye the way of YHWH, make his paths straight. 4
And the same John had his raiment of camel's hair, and a

leathern girdle about his loins; and his meat was locusts and wild honey. [5] Then went out to him Jerusalem, and all Judaea, and all the region round about Jordan, [6] And were baptized of him in Jordan, confessing their sins. [7] But when he saw many of the Pharisees and Sadducees come to his baptism, he said unto them, O generation of vipers, who hath warned you to flee from the wrath to come? [8] Bring forth therefore fruits meet for repentance: [9] And think not to say within yourselves, We have Abraham to our father: for I say unto you, that YHWH is able of these stones to raise up children unto Abraham. [10] And now also the axe is laid unto the root of the trees: therefore every tree which bringeth not forth good fruit is hewn down, and cast into the fire. [11] I indeed baptize you with water unto repentance: but he that cometh after me is mightier than I, whose shoes I am not worthy to bear: he shall baptize you with the Holy Spirit, and with fire: [12] Whose fan is in his hand, and he will throughly purge his floor, and gather his wheat into the garner; but he will burn up the chaff with unquenchable fire. (Mt 3:1-13)

Yohanan was baptizing them and hearing their confessions, he also was reproving and warning them. To let them know, because they were children of Abraham did not matter they had to become cleansed and tow the line, confess and walk right. Many of the people of Hebrew decent had the mind set, they would have everlasting life regardless of their wrongs, as long as they kept the law.

WRONG! What Yohanan said proves again we are to be obedient to YHWH's law of love, to love Him with all our heart mind and strength, and love your neighbor as your self. Most of the religious leaders in that time did not fulfill the law of love. Yahushua said unless our righteousness excide the righteousness of the Pharisees we would in no wise enter into the kingdom of heaven! Which means they will not unless they had a complete change of heart and repented. They will also have to become a complete man in Yahushua, by His spirit of favor. Remember real heart felt confession cleanses the soul.

If we confess our sins? He is faithful and just to forgive? Us! Our sins! And cleanse us! From all unrighteousness! (1John 1:9)

HalleluYah praise YHWH glory to the lamb of YHWH Yahushua the Messiah whom has made a way for all to have favor and much mercy from the Heavenly Father Yah! So we may know Him and love Him and do His will, walking in truth and the Spirit of Holiness. Because through the blood of Yahushua the Messiah we are forgiven our wrongs, and set free from all those wrong and wicked ways. Because of His work on Golgotha we are set free and no longer slave to the power of death, death no longer reigns over us in Messiah Yahushua, because He lives, we live in Him and with Him, HalleluYAH!

We all must realize the Hebrew or Jewish (Messiah / Mashiyach) is the correct name and way. Yahushua was not and is not Greek, American, African, Asian, So His name is Yahushua ha Mashiyach! When the name is translated this is how the change should be from (Yahushua to Iahushua) so in the Greek it would still have the same pronunciation as the original Hebrew and not be changed to an improper name. Remember Yahushua told the lady at the well (Salvation is of the (Jews / Yehudim) YHWH chose them to be the lineage of the Messiah Yahushua. I do know YHWH allowed His scriptures to be used to bring those who search out the complete truth, into the fold of Yahushua the Messiah. Because we all have to overcome the false doctrines and lies told us by the modern day clergy, such as the changing of the Messiah's name and the changing of the Fathers name from Yahweh to (lord thy god) which signifies no name at all. These are all deceptions, brought about by man not YHWH, we are not supposed to translate or should I say change the name of any one. When we introduce our selves and tell them our name that is what they will call us. For instance I was talking to a Spanish woman who's name is Sonia, I asked her what was her name in Spanish? she said Sonia, then I said what is your name in the English? Sonia! It never changed, that name identified her because that is who she was. The Anti–Messiah spirit is against the real name of the Father Yahweh and the real name of the Son Yahushua, because of the anti Messiah spirit, many who really believe the good news of the Apostles Matthew, Mark, Luke, and John are using an improper none authorized name that is not Yahushua the Messiah's. But another name that turns the believers against the true Messiah Yahushua which is a subtle deception, one that can destroy. The most important desire of YHWH is for use to have the mind set like Yahushua's and do the Fathers will, and that only can happen by learning of Him by the scriptures the Pentateuch, the Prophets, Psalms, Proverbs, and the Messianic writings. All these teach enlighten, reprove, and direct us into the mind set of righteousness. Which is the desire of the Father YHWH for us all to be of righteous thinking and not the other. This is why he gave us His word to learn from, to become like He is Set Apart because He is Set apart. I would also like to encourage all to seek truth daily asking Him in prayer for the truth, and He will show you and put people in your path to tell you truths you must know. Remember after the first sin when YHWH said man is like us now to know good and evil!

22 And YHWH said, Behold, the man is become as one of
us, to know good and evil: and now, lest he put forth his hand,
and take also of the tree of life, and eat, and live for ever: 23
Therefore YHWH sent him forth from the garden of Eden,
to till the ground from whence he was taken. (Gen 3:22-23)

Adam was a man made for good and not evil, he was to be fruitful and replenish the earth. YHWH did not want men to be evil but good, righteous, otherwise He would have made man good and evil. You see evil is His creation as well, YHWH made it and has the full knowledge of evils capabilities. Because when YHWH said to know good and evil, meant man is now evil as well as good. Lets search out that word (know) the first mention is in Genesis 3:5 but we are looking at context so (Gen3:22)

3045 הָעָ·ד, עַדָי [yada` /yaw·dah/] v. A primitive root: translates as "know" 645 times, "known" 105 times, "knowledge" 19 times, "perceive" 18 times, "shew" 17 times, "tell" eight times, "wist" seven times, "understand" seven times, "certainly" seven times, "acknowledge" six times, "acquaintance" six times, "consider" six times, "declare" six times, "teach" five times, and translated miscellaneously 85 times. 1 to know. 1A1 to know. 1A1A to know, learn to know. 1A1B to perceive. 1A1C to perceive and see, find out and discern. 1A1D to discriminate, distinguish. 1A1E to know by experience. 1A1F to recognise, admit, acknowledge, confess. 1A1G to consider. 1A2 to know, be acquainted_with. 1A3 to know (a person carnally). 1A4 to know how, be skilful in. 1A5 to have knowledge, be wise. 1B1 to be made known, be or become known, be revealed. 1B2 to make oneself known. 1B3 to be perceived. 1B4 to be instructed. to cause to know. 1D to cause to know. 1E 1E1 to be known. 1E2 known, one known, acquaintance (participle). 1F to make known, declare. 1G to be made known. 1H to make oneself known, reveal oneself.

To know in this instance is much like this, the mind of man is now evil as well as good! He is unpredictable unstable in his thinking, he must subdue the evil and choose righteousness, or he can choose evil and stay in death. Either way it is a choice we all have to make everyone is given free will to decide life or death.

The importance of those actions taken by YHWH should let all of us know He will not except or tolerate evil, but wants us all to be good of our own free will and desire. He has given us all free will to choose good or evil, life or death. Those who are evil will not enter in to eat from the tree of life. The reason? We are to overcome the evil and the desires of the flesh. Lust of the flesh is a destroyer, because lusting causes wrong thinking and becomes an action, we commit. Lust is what happened when Dawid a man after YHWH's own heart looked upon Bathsheba Dawid lusted after her and he was the King of Israel.

1 And it came to pass, after the year was expired, at
the time when kings go forth to battle, that David sent
Joab, and his servants with him, and all Israel; and they
destroyed the children of Ammon, and besieged Rabbah.
But David tarried still at Jerusalem. 2 And it came to pass
in an eveningtide, that David arose from off his bed, and
walked upon the roof of the king's house: and from the
roof he saw a woman washing herself; and the woman was
very beautiful to look upon. 3 And David sent and enquired
after the woman. And one said, Is not this Bathsheba the
daughter of Eliam, the wife of Uriah the Hittite?

4 And David sent messengers, and took her; and she
came in unto him, and he lay with her; for she was purified

from her uncleanness: and she returned unto her house. [5]
And the woman conceived, and sent and told David, and
said, I am with child. (2Sam 11:1-5)

Now Dawid repented but he still had to deal with the consequences of his actions. YHWH spoke through the prophet Nathan and corrected Dawid. One of the things to realize is lust was a generational curse upon his children after him, as his story tells. Even (Shalomoh / Solomon) had a strong desire toward women, which is a sign of lustfulness. He had 1000 wives and concubines. Some of his wives served the false el molech and that is what did Shalomoh in and caused him to loose YHWH's favor. Because after he sacrificed to Molech, the scriptures has very few mentions of him. I sure do love YHWH for His faithfulness, look at Abraham and YHWH's promise to him! YHWH has fulfilled all He said. He also fulfilled His promises to Dawid.

[8] Now therefore so shalt thou say unto my servant
David, Thus saith YHWH of hosts, I took thee from the
sheepcote, from following the sheep, to be ruler over my
people, over Israel: [9] And I was with thee whithersoever
thou wentest, and have cut off all thine enemies out of thy
sight, and have made thee a great name, like unto the name
of the great men that are in the earth. [10] Moreover I will
appoint a place for my people Israel, and will plant them,
that they may dwell in a place of their own, and move no
more; neither shall the children of wickedness afflict them

any more, as beforetime, [11] And as since the time that I commanded judges to be over my people Israel, and have caused thee to rest from all thine enemies. Also YHWH telleth thee that he will make thee an house. [12] And when thy days be fulfilled, and thou shalt sleep with thy fathers, I will set up thy seed after thee, which shall proceed out of thy bowels, and I will establish his kingdom. [13] He shall build an house for my name, and I will stablish the throne of his kingdom for ever. [14] I will be his father, and he shall be my son. If he commit iniquity, I will chasten him with the rod of men, and with the stripes of the children of men: [15] But my mercy shall not depart away from him, as I took it from Saul, whom I put away before thee. [16] And thine house and thy kingdom shall be established for ever before thee: thy throne shall be established for ever. [17] According to all these words, and according to all this vision, so did Nathan speak unto David! (2Sam 7:8-17)

When you read that, it is apparent YHWH was saying eternal because He is the one whom shall make it come to pass and we know He did through Yahushua the Anointed Son of YHWH.

[31] And, behold, thou shalt conceive in thy womb, and bring forth a son, and shalt call his name Yahushua. [32] He shall be great, and shall be called the Son of the Highest: and YHWH shall give unto him the throne of his father David: [33] And he shall reign over the house of Jacob for ever; and of his kingdom there shall be no end. (Luke 1:31-33)

Now it is clear YHWH does not do anything without reason and purpose, He does not waist one single movement of thought. This is why He said through the angel Gabriel:

[18] Now the birth of Yahushua the Messiah was on this
wise: When as his mother Mary was espoused to Joseph,
before they came together, she was found with child of the
Holy Spirit. [19] Then Joseph her husband, being a just man,
and not willing to make her a publick example, was minded
to put her away privily. [20] But while he thought on these
things, behold, the angel YHWH appeared unto him in a
dream, saying, Joseph, thou son of David, fear not to take
unto thee Mary thy wife: for that which is conceived in
her is of the Holy Spirit. [21] And she shall bring forth a
son, and thou shalt call his name Yahushua for he shall
save his people from their sins. [22] Now all this was done,
that it might be fulfilled which was spoken of YHWH by
the prophet, saying, [23] Behold, a virgin shall be with child,
and shall bring forth a son, and they shall call his name
Emmanuel, which being interpreted is, Elohim with us. [24]
Then Joseph being raised from sleep did as the angel of
YHWH had bidden him, and took unto him his wife: [25]
And knew her not till she had brought forth her firstborn
son: and he called his name Yahushua. (Mt1:18-25)

Now keep in mind Yahushua means YHWH is Salvation! And there is not a (J) in the Hebrew language, nor was the J in any language until the late 1600's and is only in the English language. So I will say Jehovah is an improper translation as well, it should actually be (Yahovah Nisi), or (Yahovah Yireh), As the Strong's shows us His real name: (and is the dictionary for the KJV, which is the KJV translation)

H3068 יהוה, יְהוִה [Yâhovah /yeh·ho·vaw/] 6519 occurrences; translates as 6510 times, ("GOD"/ Elohim) four times, "JEHOVAH" four times, and "variant" once.

1 the proper name of the one true God. 1A unpronounced except with the vowel pointings of 0136. Additional Information: Jehovah = "the existing One".

See that? Yahovah the proper name of the one true Elohim! He is the same YHWH!

Exodus, 11 And Mosheh said unto YHWH Elohim, Who am I, that I should go unto Pharaoh, and that I should bring forth the children of Israel out of Egypt? [12] And he said, Certainly I will be with thee; and this shall be a token unto thee, that I have sent thee: When thou hast brought forth the people out of Egypt, ye shall serve Me upon this mountain. [13] And Moses said unto YHWH, Behold, when I come unto the children of Israel, and shall say unto them, The El' of your fathers hath sent me unto you; and they shall say to me, What is his name? what shall I say unto them? [14] And YHWH said unto Moses, (I AM THAT I AM: / Eyah asure Eyah) and he said, Thus shalt thou say unto the children of Israel, (I AM / EYAH) hath sent me unto you. [15] And YHWH said moreover unto Moses, Thus shalt thou say unto the children of Israel, YHWH the Elohim of your fathers, the Elohim of Abraham, the Elohim of Isaac, and the Elohim of Jacob, hath sent me unto you: this is my name for ever, and this is my memorial unto all generations. (EX 3:11-15)

Now when a person was sent it meant he or she was under the authority of him that sent them, which means they are an extension of him who they had been sent by. Mosheh was doing as YHWH said and mighty works followed his speaking just as if YHWH Himself was right there doing it in person.

Strong's verifies this name: in the KJV dictionary.

H 3050 יָה [Yahh /yaw/] and H 1961 אֶהְיֶה, הָיָה [hayah /haw·yaw/] although the real pronunciation is (EYAH) no h sound and the (E) is silent with a drawn out (Y"Y")

Now you can ask am I a language expert? No but I have studied Hebrew teachers writings on the very subject of His true name, and that is what they say. (EYAH) is his name in Exodus, and (Yahovah) is His name in Genesis! So in all reality He is called by this name worldwide (YHWH) or Yahweh as many say. YHWH is the Father of all! All things were created by Him and Yahushua was there, the right hand of the Father, beholding His glory and doing His will in the creation of all that is was and ever will be.

1 Behold, the hand of YHWH is not shortened, that it cannot save; neither his ear heavy, that it cannot hear: (Isa 59:1)

Yahushua was there with Him in the beginning of all and is the Aleph and the Taw the author and finisher of our faith. I will remind all it is only by His spirit of holiness in us, we can come boldly to the throne of grace and judgment. If any one has not the Spirit of Holiness they will not be there in the eternal place at all. But cast out into outer darkness as the scriptures say:

1 And Yahushua answered and spake unto them again by
parables, and said, 2 The kingdom of heaven is like unto a
certain king, which made a marriage for his son,

3 And sent forth his servants to call them that were bidden
to the wedding: and they would not come. 4 Again, he sent
forth other servants, saying, Tell them which are bidden,
Behold, I have prepared my dinner: my oxen and *my* fatlings
are killed, and all things *are* ready: come unto the marriage.
5 But they made light of *it*, and went their ways, one to his
farm, another to his merchandise: 6 And the remnant took
his servants, and entreated them spitefully, and slew them. 7
But when the king heard thereof, he was wroth: and he sent
forth his armies, and destroyed those murderers, and burned
up their city. 8 Then saith he to his servants, The wedding is
ready, but they which were bidden were not worthy. 9 Go ye
therefore into the highways, and as many as ye shall find,
bid to the marriage. 10 So those servants went out into the
highways, and gathered together all as many as they found,
both bad and good: and the wedding was furnished with
guests. 11 And when the king came in to see the guests, he

saw there a man which had not on a wedding garment: [12] And he saith unto him, Friend, how camest thou in hither not having a wedding garment? And he was speechless. [13] Then said the king to the servants, Bind him hand and foot, and take him away, and cast him into outer darkness; there shall be weeping and gnashing of teeth. [14] For many are called, but few are chosen. (Mat 22:1-13)

That does signify we all must have the spirit of life and no other. The Holy Spirit is another one of His fail safes, against the false teachers and evil doers. All those who steal the spirit from another by any means will be cast out them selves. Because they are thieves and robbers, and will perish with the wicked. YHWH does not take kindly to thieves and robbers, which is why Yahushua said all that came before me were thieves and robbers.

[1] Verily, verily, I say unto you, He that entereth not by the door into the sheepfold, but climbeth up some other way, the same is a thief and a robber. [2] But he that entereth in by the door is the shepherd of the sheep. [3] To him the porter openeth; and the sheep hear his voice: and he calleth his own sheep by name, and leadeth them out. [4] And when he putteth forth his own sheep, he goeth before them, and the sheep follow him: for they know his voice. [5] And a stranger will they not follow, but will flee from him: for they know not the voice of strangers. [6] This parable spake Yahushua unto them: but they understood not what things they were which he spake unto them. [7] Then said Yahushua

unto them again, Verily, verily, I say unto you, I am the door
of the sheep. [8] All that ever came before me are thieves and
robbers: but the sheep did not hear them. [9] I am the door:
by me if any man enter in, he shall be saved, and shall go in
and out, and find pasture. [10] The thief cometh not, but for to
steal, and to kill, and to destroy: I am come that they might
have life, and that they might have it more abundantly.
[11] I am the good shepherd: the good shepherd giveth his
life for the sheep. (John 10:1-11). (Thieves and robbers)

That shows use there is no other way into the kingdom but by Yahushua and grace of YHWH through Him. Those that steal and take from another by any other means will perish. All of those ministers who are in the anti-messiah spirit are told to take the gifts of others mainly those in Yahushua. Those who use drug sorcery and mind control drugs, and those who steal from little children, those who steal by means of rape of any one male or female they will not enter into the kingdom, but will be cast out into outer darkness as well. Remember adultery is a sin and is death, so is selling any gift of the Holy Spirit, that gift is not to be sold for monies or at any price. I'm telling this to you? Because not many people realize they have even been victimized, or had dealings with those who steal from believers. And if you are in the anti Messiah spirit no one will try to steal that gift because even those in familiar spirits do not worry about you because they are very much alike. Witches and wizards do not fear that spirit, it is only the word they do not like to deal with, it makes them angry because the word condemns all who are doing against it. None the less, those in Yahushua are targets and have to guard their gift of life from all who do not have that gift. The false spirit they have tells them to take your gift. You want proof, ok let us look at the first original apostles, did they all die of old age or by crucifixion?

Andrew was crucified, Bartholomew was beaten then crucified, James son of Alpheus was stoned to death, James son of Zebedee was beheaded. With John, they tried to kill him by putting him in boiling oil. He was not marked or hurt. Despite all their attempts, he was not put to death but only exiled to Patmos. There, he wrote the book of Revelation. He was the only apostle not murdered by man's hand, what really happened to him is only known by YHWH. Judas (not Iscariot) was stoned to death, Matthew was speared to death, Peter was crucified upside down, Phillip was crucified, Simon was crucified, Thomas was speared to death, and Matthias was also speared to death.

(Source: Fox's book of Martyrs)

The reason was so the Roman Catholics could take their gifts from them, Yahushua said they hated me they will hate you also. Most of the worldly religions are not of the real spirit, Yahushua the Messiah but of the Roman Catholic Anti Messiah spirit, that is against Yahushua and the Father YHWH. And almost all the worlds' religions are of the Roman Catholic tree. Catholicism is the beginning of the tree of all the Christian denominations from Lutheranism, Methodism, Mormonism, Jehovah witnesses and all the denominations that use the scriptures, but keep mans day of worship, mans feasts and holy days. Now keep in mind many of those Jewish were not all believers on Messiah but on the Father YHWH only, they would be considered the same as today's Orthodox Jewish! Who believe in the Father but not the Son Yahushua and many do not believe the Messiah came yet. They are called orthodox because they adhear to the Pentateuch and what is called by many the Old Testament writings. In this day and age many people around the world are disillusioned by what they know to be the truth taught them by the modern day religious leaders. Their ideas are very off the scripture path, and have many teachings that go against what the scriptures say. Why because the spirit that leads them is not of Yahushua but another, that spirit is teaching everyone in that belief system incorrectly and away from YHWH's true way, Yahushua the Messiah! You really need to get this people? Any spirit! That teaches contrary to or away from the scriptures is a false spirit.

34 Verily I say unto you, this generation shall not pass, till
all these things be fulfilled.

35 Heaven and earth shall pass away, but my words shall
not pass away. (Mat 24:34-35) (Mar 13:31), (Luke 21:33)

10 But the day of the Master will come as a thief in the
night; in the which the heavens shall pass away with a great

noise, and the elements shall melt with fervent heat, the earth also and the works that are therein shall be burned up. (2Pet 3:10)

To some it is as plain as the nose on their face and others cannot see or comprehend, the scriptures are all one writing and Yahushua is the completion of what the Father desired from the beginning after Adam and Eve we all were put into death by sin. In other words Yahushua completes the law in us all who are His, and who have Him in their hearts.

17 Think not that I am come to destroy the law, or the
prophets: I am not come to destroy, but to fulfil. 18 For verily
I say unto you, Till heaven and earth pass, one jot or one
tittle shall in no wise pass from the law, till all be fulfilled.
(Mat 5:17-18)

Also the scriptures reveal to us these things, regularly by His Spirit. (He completed the scriptures) and also is the (completion of man) to become sons of YHWH. The Pentateuch, the Prophets, the Psalms, Proverbs, Minor Prophets, then the Messianic scriptures which is the renewed covenant writings of mans salvation in YHWH through His Son Yahushua. Then the Epistles, and the Revelation of Yohanan / John, all which are of the inspiration of YHWH through the word of YHWH our Yahushua! HalleluYah!

8 But there is a spirit in man: and the inspiration of El
Shaddai giveth them understanding. 9 Great men are not

always wise: neither do the aged understand judgment. (Job 32:8-9)

16 All scripture is given by inspiration of YHWH, and is profitable for doctrine, for reproof, for correction, for instruction in righteousness: (2Tim 3:16)

27 But the anointing which ye have received of him abideth in you, and ye need not that any man teach you: but as the same anointing teacheth you of all things, and is truth, and is no lie, and even as it hath taught you, ye shall abide in him. (1John 2:27)

18 We know that whosoever is born of Elohim sinneth
not; but he that is begotten of YHWH keepeth himself,
and that wicked one toucheth him not. 19 And we know
that we are of YHWH, and the whole world lieth in
wickedness. 20 And we know that the Son of YHWH is
come, and hath given us an understanding, that we may
know him that is true, and we are in him that is true, even
in his Son Yahushua ha Mashiyach. This is the true Elohim,
(1John 5:18-20)

Now I know it may be hard for many to take because all our lives we have been taught another way or another name or doctrine. But the truth is, just because we have been deceived by others and have made the mistake of doing as those in the anti-Messiah spirit, does not mean we cannot change. Even if you have been baptized in to the (anti –Messiah) spirit, it is not to late to make a change and do according to YHWH's word and will. Pray daily for

YHWH's truth in Yahushua the beloved Son! And learn of Him in all the scriptures cover to cover. Many people will say that is your interpretation, but I asure you, we are to have the same doctrinal knowledge, because He who inspired the scriptures desires us to be as He is! A spiritual being walking with Him in truth and HIS Holiness!

Do you really think YHWH is going to say well it's ok that you are in a different spirit than mine, and you did not understand what I told you to do from my words, and it 's ok that you were deceived and listening to the wrong spirit! It's ok you stole from my servant because you were deceived, into thinking you were doing gods will instead of mine, and it's ok that you do not know what name to call me, or it's ok for you to honor mans ways instead of mine. And the list goes on and on!! YHWH is the one we are to be learning of and from by the spirit of Yahushua the El of our Salvation!

20And we know that the Son of Elohim has come and has given us an understanding, so that we might know the true One. And we are in the true One, in His Son Yahushua the Messiah. This is the true Elohim and everlasting life. (1John 5:20)

To many people have the idea YHWH the Father and Yahushua the Son are just going to roll over and let them have their own way. Many say and think just because HE KNOWS MY HEART He will give them a green light because they meant well, and were deceived, by the preacher? Or maybe he will have pity on all those who rejected Him and His words for mans. Then he may say, sure come on in rest relax do what ever you would like? Yes I sent my word? and my spirit? and My son so you could be deceived and worship false gods and do it your own way! COME ON people, YHWH will not be mocked or made to do what you or I want! If that was true about Him knowing you and your heart the way many say, why would He have given you and I the scriptures to learn from and His spirit of life to be taught by. Why would He have given His beloved Son's blood so He could shower us with loving kindness and tender mercies? And how can you say you even know Him if you do not keep His word and way, like His proclaimed Sabbath and His Holy Feasts? And why do so many disregard the scriptures they do not want to do or be obedient to? Many have heard in their spirit from YHWH the way they are doing those things were wrong! But disregarded what they heard because everybody does it that way! So search it out seek the real truth from Him who is all in all? Question the preacher, question what you know is wrong, be a seeker of HIS ways not mans. His ways lead to life, mans ways lead to death. Only His way is life everlasting! One of the worst mistakes man makes is when they think they know it all. Then any other truth cannot benefit them, but cause condemnation and anger. Sounds like the Pharisees and the Sadducees!

12 There is a way which seems right unto a man, but the end thereof are the ways of death. (Pr 14:12)

Yahushua reproved them by the scriptures they lived by and used to make others do as they said, those religious men made their living from the scriptures. They all had more than any average person as the scripture show us.

[23] Woe unto you, scribes and Pharisees, hypocrites! for ye pay tithe of mint and anise and cummin, and have omitted the weightier *matters* of the law, judgment, mercy, and faith: these ought ye to have done, and not to leave the other undone. (Mat 23:23)

[42] But woe unto you, Pharisees! for ye tithe mint and rue and all manner of herbs, and pass over judgment and the love of Elohim: these ought ye to have done, and not to leave the other undone. [43] Woe unto you, Pharisees! for ye love the uppermost seats in the synagogues, and greetings in the markets. [44] Woe unto you, scribes and Pharisees, hypocrites! for ye are as graves which appear not, and the men that walk over them are not aware of them. (Luke 11:42-44)

Back in those days many people could not afford to even have many of those spices.

[43] And he called unto him his disciples, and saith unto them, Verily I say unto you, That this poor widow hath cast more in, than all they which have cast into the treasury: [44] For all they did cast in of their abundance; but she of her want did cast in all that she had, even all her living. (Mark 12:43-44) and also (Luke 21:3)

Either way you see the religious leaders had no lack for anything, food, clothing, housing and coin or spices, ect. Well you get the idea, and why was that, the people were being obedient to YHWH's word, and many were poor folk. Yahushua reproved them to the point of their, blind shame, because they had knowledge but did not share or teach the real desire of YHWH the Father to those they ministered to. As the scripture says they burdened them and took without mercy!

13 But woe unto you, scribes and Pharisees, hypocrites! for ye shut up the kingdom of heaven against men: for ye neither go in yourselves, neither suffer ye them that are entering to
go in. 14 Woe unto you, scribes and Pharisees, hypocrites! for ye devour widows' houses, and for a pretence make long prayer: therefore ye shall receive the greater damnation.
15 Woe unto you, scribes and Pharisees, hypocrites! for ye compass sea and land to make one proselyte, and when he is made, ye make him twofold more the child of hell than yourselves. (Mat 23:13-15) also (Mar 12:40) & (Luke 20:47)

Yahushua was angry at those religious leaders of the masses then, well what do you think He would say about today's religious leaders? The scriptures say those who are in ministry and make their living from it are going to be held accountable to higher level than those of the folds. When man take a scriptural truth and adds to it for his own agenda it becomes a lie. What is replacement theology?

[20] Notwithstanding I have a few things against thee, because thou sufferest that woman Jezebel, which calleth herself a prophetess, to teach and to seduce my servants to commit fornication, and to eat things sacrificed unto idols. [21] And I gave her space to repent of her fornication; and she repented not. [22] Behold, I will cast her into a bed, and them that commit adultery with her into great tribulation, except they repent of their deeds. [23] And I will kill her children with death; and all the Assemblies shall know that I am he which searcheth the reins and hearts: and I will give unto every one of you according to your works. (Rev 2:20)

Yahushua also said except our righteousness exceed the righteousness of the Pharisees and Sadducees and Scribes we will in no ways enter into the kingdom of Heaven.

[17] Think not that I am come to destroy the law, or the prophets: I am not come to destroy, but to fulfil. [18] For verily I say unto you, Till heaven and earth pass, one jot or one tittle shall in no wise pass from the law, till all be fulfilled. [19] Whosoever therefore shall break one of these least commandments, and shall teach men so, he shall be called the least in the kingdom of heaven: but whosoever shall do and teach them, the same shall be called great in the kingdom of heaven. [20] For I say unto you, That except your righteousness shall exceed the righteousness of the scribes and Pharisees, ye shall in no case enter into the kingdom of heaven. (Mat 5:17-20).

It is very important to see the fundamental truth of scripture, but is of the utmost importance to do and keep the word as YHWH intended. A lot of the modern day religious leaders teach primarily new testament or away from Torah, and the prophets. Many years ago I was talking to a church leader about more people coming to the meetings, one thing lead to another and he told me not to teach from the law or the Torah, when I asked why he said when you do they have questions you should not answer, because when you do they will not come back. At that time in my walk I did not get the full meaning of that statement, but now I really do understand the word is one book of many writings and all of them are His instruction of righteousness. All the scripture from Matthew to revelation is all about the refining of the original writings of Mosheh, everything in the Messianic writings is an explanation of Torah. The revelations of their writings is what has given us a better understanding into the correct way of seeing, the scriptures, and expounding them for our understanding. Why? So we can get in the right mind set of YHWH, if you really look at what they are saying! You can see they all are referring to the Torah, the Prophets, many times Psalms, even Proverbs. So you see all latest scripture refers to what many call the Old Testament. WHY? because Yahushua the Messiah is the completion of the Torah, HalleluYah. We are to become complete in Yahushua's likeness and no other! We are to know the Torah and the Prophets, the

Psalms and Proverbs, the Songs of Shalomoh, Ecclesiastes. Because He is in there, the word is in there. YHWH has shown to us who believe we must seek Yahushua His Messiah who takes all the sins of the world upon Himself to free mankind from the power of lies and death. I do realize a matter of truth, concerning the modern days religions of Christianity, YHWH allowed it to bring those through into His Beloved Son Yahushua the Messiah. He was looking at those who persevered and did not stop at the doctrine of easy beliefs. I know there is a lot of Christians out there with many unanswered questions about the old testament. Things they have read and have no clearness of, and the spirit in them leaves it unanswered and blank. Well that is when you need to pray for the real truth and seek the answer from Him who made all things.

[13] Howbeit when he, the Spirit of truth, is come, he will guide you into all truth: for he shall not speak of himself; but whatsoever he shall hear, that shall he speak: and he will shew you things to come. [14] He shall glorify me: for he shall receive of mine, and shall shew it unto you.(John 16:13-14)

[17] Sanctify them through thy truth: thy word is truth. [18] As thou hast sent me into the world, even so have I also sent them into the world. [19] And for their sakes I sanctify myself, that they also might be sanctified through the truth.(John 17:17-19)

[31] Then said Yahushua to those Jews which believed on him, If ye continue in my word, then are ye my

disciples indeed; [32] And ye shall know the truth, and the truth shall make you free. (John 8:31-32)

The word truth only has one meaning in Hebrew, Greek, English all languages! The correct way, moral integrity, the truth of a matter, either way truth is the opposite of lie! And a lie has no place in truth, therefore the lie is always brought to light and cast down, be it immediately or in a circumference of time.

[25] In meekness instructing those that oppose themselves; if YHWH peradventure will give them repentance to the acknowledging of the truth; [26] And that they may recover themselves out of the snare of the devil, who are taken captive by him at his will. (2Tim 2:25-26)

How many of us who believe disregard the truth when we see it or hear it because it seems to be foreign to us, or is not what we had been taught. Realize this! The end times are near and there are many false doctrines which are doctrines of demons and devils. They are doctrines that lead to ultimate death, even though they sound like truth. Many good believers are following those doctrines of death un aware, it is called deception, mans deception. And is completely scriptural:

[1] Now the Spirit speaketh expressly, that in the latter times some shall depart from the faith, giving heed to seducing spirits, and doctrines of devils; [2] Speaking lies in hypocrisy; having their conscience seared with a hot iron; [3] Forbidding to marry, and commanding to abstain from

meats, which YHWH hath created to be received with thanksgiving of them which believe and know the truth. (1Tim 4:1-3)

[20] Wherefore if ye be dead with Messiah from the rudiments of the world, why, as though living in the world, are ye subject to ordinances, [21] (Touch not; taste not; handle not; [22] Which all are to perish with the using;) after the commandments and doctrines of men? [23] Which things have indeed a shew of wisdom in will worship, and humility, and neglecting of the body; not in any honour to the satisfying of the flesh. (Col 2:20-23)

The truth is they already have disappeared from the doctrines of today's religiosity, touch not the unclean things, eat no unclean thing, handle not or have nothing to do with wrong affiliations. Discipline in the word is becoming very unheard of these days, because the world is changing from righteous beliefs to what ever you want and believe, and all ways lead to heaven! Nothing could be farther from the truth, the world is doing what the scriptures has been saying. Calling evil good and good evil, and even doing things that are completely wrong against mankind, in secret and public. The television commercials are telling every one how wrong it is to speak out publicly against the wrongs being forced upon people in this nation. The celebrities and rich are able to by freedoms from their wrongs, real justice seems to be like a discarded vehicle not used in the court systems. Justice should be first, truth should prevail, not lies and technicalities. I do believe you get my point on that issue, for criminals to win by default is not justice but injustice. This is what the world is coming to, not what is right or wrong but what ever can be gotten away with. All verifiable reason of proof, the end time is very near. I also believe 911 was a two minute warning, a countdown has begun for those who seek His truth and live by it. The times are already showing signs of birth pains, catastrophes world wide, wars and rumors of wars. The whole world is seeing these events and many are ignoring them even excusing those signs as something else.

[1] I charge thee therefore before YHWH, and the Master
Yahushua ha Messiah, who shall judge the quick and the
dead at his appearing and his kingdom; [2] Preach the word;
be instant in season, out of season; reprove, rebuke, exhort
with all longsuffering and doctrine. [3] For the time will come
when they will not endure sound doctrine; but after their
own lusts shall they heap to themselves teachers, having
itching ears; [4] And they shall turn away their ears from the
truth, and shall be turned unto fables. (2Tim 4:1-4)

1 But there were false prophets also among the people,
even as there shall be false teachers among you, who
privily shall bring in damnable heresies, even denying the
Savior that bought them, and bring upon themselves swift
destruction. [2] And many shall follow their pernicious ways
by reason of whom the way of truth shall be evil spoken
of. [3] And through covetousness shall they with feigned

words make merchandise of you: whose judgment now of
a long time lingereth not, and their damnation slumbereth
not. 4 For if YHWH spared not the angels that sinned, but
cast them down to hell, and delivered them into chains
of darkness, to be reserved unto judgment; 5 And spared
not the old world, but saved Noah the eighth person, a
preacher of righteousness, bringing in the flood upon the
world of the unholy; 6 And turning the cities of Sodom and
Gomorrah into ashes condemned them with an overthrow,
making them an ensample unto those that after should
live unrighteous; 7 And delivered just Lot, vexed with the
filthy conversation of the wicked: 8 (For that righteous
man dwelling among them, in seeing and hearing, vexed
his righteous soul from day to day with their unlawful
deeds;) 9 The Master knoweth how to deliver the righteous
out of temptations, and to reserve the unjust unto the
day of judgment to be punished: 10 But chiefly them that
walk after the flesh in the lust of uncleanness, and despise
government Presumptuous are they, selfwilled, they are not
afraid to speak evil of dignities. 11 Whereas angels, which
are greater in power and might, bring not railing accusation
against them before the Master. 12 But these, as natural
brute beasts, made to be taken and destroyed, speak evil
of the things that they understand not; and shall utterly
perish in their own corruption; 13 And shall receive the
reward of unrighteousness, as they that count it pleasure to
riot in the day time. Spots they are and blemishes, sporting

themselves with their own deceivings while they feast with you; [14] Having eyes full of adultery and that cannot cease from sin; beguiling unstable souls: an heart they have exercised with covetous practices; cursed children: [15] Which have forsaken the right way, and are gone astray, following the way of Balaam the son of Bosor, who loved the wages of unrighteousness; [16] But was rebuked for his iniquity: the dumb ass speaking with man's voice forbad the madness of the prophet. [17] These are wells without water, clouds that are carried with a tempest; to whom the mist of darkness is reserved for ever. [18] For when they speak great swelling words of vanity, they allure through the lusts of the flesh, through much wantonness, those that were clean escaped from them who live in error. [19] While they promise them liberty, they themselves are the servants of corruption: for of whom a man is overcome, of the same is he brought in bondage. [20] For if after they have escaped the pollutions of the world through the knowledge of the Master and Saviour Messiah Yahushua, they are again entangled therein, and overcome, the latter end is worse with them than the beginning.

[21] For it had been better for them not to have known the way of righteousness, than, after they have known it, to turn from the holy commandment delivered unto them. [22] But it is happened unto them according to the true proverb, the dog is turned to his own vomit again; and the sow that was washed to her wallowing in the mire. (2Pet 2)

Those things Peter wrote about in that Epistle have already come to pass. It is a real eye opener, because it sounds so much like many religious organization in this modern times. With what they call unichurches where all ways are accepted and all doctrines are allowed to be taught. In this nation church is big business they make lots of money, most are tax exempt. Remember what James said about true religion:

27 Pure religion and undefiled before Elohim and the Father is this, To visit the fatherless and widows in their affliction, and to keep himself unspotted from the world. (Jm1:27)

Many of the things I have been through taught me lessons concerning religion in today's modern churches. I will also say they have not all been good memories. When you have a question they do not want to answer or deal with, most of the clergy will do their best to avoid or say they have no time for that now. I have met many very nice and seemly concerned Christian ministers in my days as a Christian, but the spirit in them has made most all of them do against me, in speaking or deed, claiming against me to try to take of my gift. So you see that is why those in Yahushua have to be careful where they congregate or assemble at, because when you go into a church and become apart of that organization, your gifting becomes apart of that mix, and you give full authority to the leaders of that church over you and your gifting. You also become a partaker in the works and doctrine of said church. I say this because of my experiences in past times as a Christian believer. You might ask am I against Christians? No I am not, there are millions and millions of people in the flocks of Christianity that have no idea, because of deception and bad teachings of the scriptures. YHWH has set the course for all of us who believe in Him and His Son Yahushua who is the Anointed one, the only Messiah.

22 Who is a liar but he that denieth that Yahushua is the Messiah? He is anti-Messiah, that denieth the Father and the Son. 23 Whosoever denieth the Son, the same hath not the Father: (but) he that acknowledgeth the Son hath the Father also. (1John 2:22-23)

This is why His name is so important to us who believe the scriptures. Now many people may say that is not the way you say His name but I believe, when you are shown His name and the light gets brighter in your mind when you see and truly realize that He is showing you that. Like Yehowshuwa, Yeshua, Yahshua, Yehoshua, Yahushua, these would be considered acceptable since it is of the real pronunciation of His real name. Most importantly, we all must be baptized into the real name as we hear it from Him and keep His real true way, and do the will of the Father in Heaven YHWH. It is a different learning curve but well worth the time and effort. Some many years ago I was going to be a Christian minister as I studied and learned, I had many hindrances, and trials. During that learning time I was asking for truth every day, and I was presented with truth. You see when I made the decision to become a minister of His word I heard Him say, will you be a minister like them or are you going to do it My way? I was astounded. What? Other way? He then told me other things but I said I wanted to do it His way not my own, then He said to seek the truth, look beyond what is seen, just keep asking for truth and it will come, and it did as I asked. The real question was accepting what I was learning since those things were not in the norm, compared to what was going on in the religious circles I had already known. I had been a believer in (the Father then called god) all my life as a little child in a orphanage I believed, many of the care givers would read the scriptures to us, mainly the good news of Matthew, Mark, Luke, and John. They make very good children's stories and make a lot of good questions from us little ones then. Matthew and Luke are the best because they explain in more detail, my actual favorite is the book of Matthew. And as a child I had many things happen to me, it seemed as though evil attacked me most all of my life, I believe that happens to all the believers in some form or another. Mainly it seems as if the evil is trying to make the believers quit or turn away, and give up.

But this I will say we all have the testimony of Yahushua and His grace in our lives growing up and coming into the fold. One of my biggest problems was Christian ministers and grown up believers, and those in familiar spirits, all coming after me thinking they were doing their god a service. Yahushua kept me safe all my life despite all the efforts of those against me. I also realize I'm not the only person on the earth with such a testimony, many go through extraordinary times and with overwhelming circumstances and just like me are still alive only because YHWH's love and mercy. His immense faithfulness to fulfill all His promises to those who are His. Make no mistake YHWH is able to keep His from being destroyed by their enemy, be it man or bad spirits. Which seems as though men only really have one common enemy other than another man. The spirits of darkness, because they know the truth will put an end to them and their destruction of mankind. Yahushua's deliverance is freedom from all the works of darkness, those in religiosity are still being deceived, in false light and have not been delivered from the hidden things of darkness. That means they are still being used by those false spirits, to be a force against those in real truth. Because there is a truth that sounds good to men but is not, and there is a truth many reject because of past teachings, the real truth is rejected. Keep in your mind real truth when you learn it, and it will never forsake you. Yahushua said they hated me without cause, they will hate you also. Many in the past choose to be in another religion not the true way because they have deemed it to hard of a walk. And so because of their decision they will not reap Yahushua's reward but mans, as the word does says.

[24] Then said Yahushua unto his disciples, If any man will come after me, let him deny himself, and take up his cross, and follow me. [25] For whosoever will save his life shall lose it: and whosoever will lose his life for my sake shall find it. [26] For what is a man profited, if he shall gain the whole world, and lose his own soul? or what shall a man give in exchange for his soul? [27] For the Son of man shall come in the glory of his Father with his angels; and then he shall reward every man according to his works. [28] Verily I say unto you, There be some standing here, which shall not taste of death, till they see the Son of man coming in his kingdom. (Mat 16:24-28)

[8] Now he that planteth and he that watereth are one: and every man shall receive his own reward according to his own labour. (1Cor 3:8)

The reward for false prophets is death, and the reward for false ministers and or teachers is according to their works. False teachers mislead or use the position for personal gain, they are still going to be held accountable to a higher level. Wolves in sheep's clothing, the hireling those who use YHWH's word to deceive destroy, and steal, are considered thieves and robbers, those will be cast out into outer darkness with the dogs.

[14] Blessed are they that do his Commandments that they may have right to the tree of life, and may enter in through the gates into the city. [15] For without are dogs, and

sorcerers, and whoremongers, and murderers, and idolaters, and whosoever loveth and maketh a lie. (Rev 22:14-15)

[14] But cursed be the deceiver, which hath in his flock a male, and voweth, and sacrificeth unto YHWH a corrupt thing: for I am a great King, saith YHWH of hosts, and my name is dreadful among the heathen. (Mal 1:14)

A deceiver is cursed in any case. You cannot deceive YHWH, but those who deceive their brother are also cursed because His word says so, and is the same as a false witness. Remember you cannot do against his word, it is automatic, you are under the blessing or the cursing, some ministers' think they can out smart YHWH's word but it will not allow them victory over His people. In the end those who used His word for the destruction of His people, will not like the end result in their future paradise. I must tell you He is one, YHWH is thee one who is and who was and is to come! Seek the revelation of Yahushua the Son and the revelation of the Father YHWH.

[17] And when they saw him, they worshipped him: but some doubted. [18] And Yahushua came and spake unto them, saying, All power is given unto me in heaven and in earth. [19] Go ye therefore, and teach all nations, baptizing them in the name of the Father, and of the Son, and of the Holy Spirit: [20] Teaching them to observe all things whatsoever I have commanded you: and, lo, I am with you alway, even unto the end of the world. Amen. (Mat 28:17-20)

There is a reason for the way Yahushua said baptizing them in the name of the Father, and of the Son, and of the Holy Spirit: Yahushua also said I come in my Fathers name. He also said if you have seen Me you have seen the Father also: In the old days a man would send another man one of his servants or son maybe a sister or brother to give a message. The one receiving the message always would ask by what name do you come.

It is the same as saying by what authority, or whose protection are they under. And so the name meant everything when relaying the message. Yahushua said to baptize all in the name of the Father, Son, and Holy Spirit which also is the same as by the power and authority of the Father, Son, and Holy Spirit. The name we should use to relay that authority to others in the baptism? Yahushua ha Mashiyach! So you see we should pronounce it like this: when we baptize a new brother or sister, I baptize you by the power and authority of the Father and the Son and the Holy Spirit in the Name of Yahushua the Messiah! After you baptize them it is important for the person speaking this over the new brother or sister to lay hands on them, and the elders if any that are in Yahushua and speak what YHWH puts on their heart to say over them, the gift of the Holy Spirit, protection from the wicked spirits and guidance, and ect. It is also important to be baptized by a man who is already in Yahushua the Messiah. I say this because I had talked with many women who said they baptized themselves this is not biblical or proper. The scriptures say these three agree in one:

[6] This is he that came by water and blood, even Messiah Yahushua; not by water only, but by water and blood. And it is the Spirit that beareth witness, because the Spirit is truth. [7] For there are three that bear record in heaven, the Father, the Word, and the Holy Spirit: and these three are one. [8] And there are three that bear witness in earth, the Spirit, and the water, and the blood: and these three agree in one. (1John 5:6-8 KJV)- In the earth man they agree, in one.

Remember we are made from the earth, so we must have the witness in us by His Spirit of life and light. But we also must have the servant of Yahushua pronounce this over us by the direction of the spirit of life who is YHWH's Yahushua. If you do not do according to scripture then it will not count because you will not be obeying the word of YHWH or scriptures but the replacement theology spirit. If any man or any spirit directs you to become baptized in any other name other than Yahushua, it is not the spirit of Him who wrote the scriptures, but another which means a false spirit, the one who is against YHWH the Father and Yahushua the Son. Also it is important to let you know, let no strangers or other brothers and or sisters lay hands on the new family member unless you are absolutely sure they are of the same baptism of YHWH's salvation, and no other. Many people that have the other spirits will speak wrong things that can cause confusion and deception to the new brother or sister. Now if there is a married couple man and wife, the servant of Yahushua should baptize the man and the man should baptize the wife with the servants assistance of course. Keep in mind these things are important for your future walk with YHWH the Father to be unhindered by wicked or evil spirits that will try you even destroy you if it can. The true secret is always put your trust in the word and YHWH use it as your guide, anything you hear in the spirit must line up with His word completely. Remember the evil one knows the scriptures also and will try you in them, but remember the wrong things they did in the scriptures, do not do! The right things do and continue in them. Those things were written so we could see they made mistakes, and the real proof YHWH does not show partiality, He shows the good and the bad. So we are to learn from their mistakes as they did. He will honor His word and will not go against it, because Yahushua the Messiah is the word. Also do not give up persevere, because a righteous man may fall seven times, so stand up, confess and repent, dust your self off and keep on keeping on. Remember this scripture, memorize it completely:

9 If we confess our sins, he is faithful and just to forgive us *our* sins, and to cleanse us from all unrighteousness. (1John 1:9)

Now another key principle is scripture memorization, it is of the utmost importance to put the scriptures in the memory vault (Your HEART). Most times it is hard to do but you will eventually get the meaning and be able to speak it verbatim, then you will own that scripture when you get the (revelation, understanding) of the verse or verses. Here are some that will show you the true way of salvation in Yahushua, these are commandments as Yahushua said them and the Apostles. (John 3:3, 3:5, Rom 10:9-12, 10:13, Mat 28:18-20, 1Jn 5:18-21, 1Jn 2:27, 1Jn 2:22-24) Those scriptures will help you remember key things that will stay with you all your days here and eternal, and it is important to memorize them in the real name, Yahushua the Messiah! It is also a must and really good to read the scriptures every day, ask in prayer for truth and enlightenment of His word.

[1] I am sought of them that asked not for me; I am found
of them that sought me not: I said, Here I am, Here I am,
unto a nation that was not called by my name. [2] I have
spread out my hands all the day unto a rebellious people,
which walketh in a waythat was not good, after their own
thoughts; [3] A people that provoketh me to anger continually
to my face; that sacrificeth in gardens, and burneth incense
upon altars of brick; [4] Which remain among the graves, and
lodge in the monuments, which eat swine's flesh, and broth
of abominable things is in their vessels; [5] Which say, Stand
by thyself, come not near to me; for I am holier than thou.
These are a smoke in my nose a fire that burneth all the day.
[6] Behold, it is written before me: I will not keep silence, but
will recompense, even recompense into their bosom, [7] Your

iniquities, and the iniquities of your fathers together, saith
Yahweh, which have burned incense upon the mountains,
and blasphemed me upon the hills: therefore will I measure
their former work into their bosom.[8] Thus saith Yahweh, As
the new wine is found in the cluster, and one saith, Destroy
it not; for a blessing is in it: so will I do for my servants'
sakes, that I may not destroy them all. [9] And I will bring
forth a seed out of Jacob, and out of Yudah an inheritor
of my mountains: and mine elect shall inherit it, and my
servants shall dwell there. [10] And (Sharon / the plain) shall
be a fold of flocks, and the valley of Achor a place for the
herds to lie down in, for my people that have sought me.[11]
But ye are they that forsake YHWH, that forget my holy
mountain, that prepare a table for that (troop / Gad) , and
that furnish the drink offering unto that (number / Meni).
[12] Therefore will I number you to the sword, and ye shall all
bow down to the slaughter: because when I called, ye did
not answer; when I spake, ye did not hear; but did evil before
mine eyes, and did choose that wherein I delighted not. [13]
Therefore thus saith YHWH, Behold, my servants shall eat,
but ye shall be hungry: behold, my servants shall drink, but
ye shall be thirsty: behold, my servants shall rejoice, but ye
shall be ashamed: [14] Behold, my servants shall sing for joy
of heart, but ye shall cry for sorrow of heart, and shall howl
for vexation of spirit. [15] And ye shall leave your name for
a curse unto my chosen: for I YHWH shall slay thee, and
call his servants by another name: [16] That he who blesseth

himself in the earth shall bless himself in the Elohim of truth; and he that sweareth in the earth shall swear by the Elohim of truth; because the former troubles are forgotten, and because they are hid from mine eyes.[17] For, behold, I create new heavens and a new earth: and the former shall not be remembered, nor come into mind. [18] But be ye glad and rejoice for ever in that which I create: for, behold, I create Yerushalayim a rejoicing, and her people a joy. [19] And I will rejoice in Yerushalayim, and joy in my people: and the voice of weeping shall be no more heard in her, nor the voice of crying. [20] There shall be no more thence an infant of days, nor an old man that hath not filled his days: for the child shall die an hundred years old; but the sinner being an hundred years old shall be accursed. [21] And they shall build houses, and inhabit them; and they shall plant vineyards, and eat the fruit of them. [22] They shall not build, and another inhabit; they shall not plant, and another eat: for as the days of a tree are the days of my people, and mine elect shall long enjoy the work of their hands. [23] They shall not labour in vain, nor bring forth for trouble; for they are the seed of the blessed of YHWH, and their offspring with them. [24] And it shall come to pass, that before they call, I will answer; and while they are yet speaking, I will hear. [25] The wolf and the lamb shall feed together, and the lion shall eat straw like the bullock: and dust shall be the serpent's meat. They shall not hurt nor destroy in all my holy mountain, saith Yahweh of Host Most High. (Isaiah / Yeshayahu 65)

Now when you read these verses keep in mind who YHWH is referring to as a people not called by His name. These are the people who found Him or His word who took His word for themselves and used it for their own, this is when they did replacement theology to be a righteous people, these were the heathen. Different nations that new Him not but found Him, who sought after Him, and found the most High. But did they really find Him, or did they use His word. What about the nations that took Yisra'el captive? By Yisra'el being captive by other nations those nations were changed many people in their midst became believers on Him. But YHWH is not speaking of them only but every one who believes on His word, these are them who believe His word but changed it. Yeshayahu was speaking future not present, but eternal when he said they would not be feed, because they did not keep HIS way but another.

YHWH is not talking of those who sought after Him but another! You see Gad is a false god or another mighty one.

H 1171 בַּעַל גָּד [Ba`al, Gad /bah·al gawd/] From H1168 Three occurrences; translates as "Baalgad" three times. 1 a city noted for Baal-worship, located at the most northern or northwestern point to which Joshua's victories extended. Additional Information: Baal-gad = "lord of fortune"

This is where the term and word god came from Gad or the heathen god of fortune.

H 1168 בַּעַל [Ba`al /bah·al/] Same as H 1167, 80 occurrences; translates as "Baal" 62 times, and "Baalim" 18 times. 1 supreme male divinity of the Phoenicians or Canaanites. 2 a Reubenite. 3 the son of Jehiel and grandfather of Saul. 4 a town of Simeon, probably identical to Baalath-beer. Additional Information: Baal = "lord"

H 1167 בַּעַל, בַּעַל [ba`al /bah·al/] 82 occurrences; translates as "man" 25 times, "owner" 14 times, "husband" 11 times, "have" seven times, "master" five times, "man given" twice, "adversary" once, "archers" once, "babbler, once, "bird, once, "captain" once, "confederate, once, and translated miscellaneously 12 times. 1 owner, husband, lord. 1A owner. 1B a husband. 1C citizens, inhabitants. 1D rulers, lords. 1E (noun of relationship used to characterise—ie, master of dreams). 1F lord (used of foreign gods).

H 4507 מְנִי [Mâniy /men·ee/] translates as "number" once. 1 god of fate who the Jews worshipped in Babylonia. Additional Information: Meni = "fate" or "fortune"

Now (Meni) was a false elohim that the Jews were made to worship in captivity. But those who know His name and follow Him Yahweh's Yahushua, and those under His eternal promise before Yahushua's ascension into the heavens. His elect and His servants, and His people that sought Him will be taken care of and blessed by YHWH. But those following false gods and who do not keep His way and do not His will shall perish because Yahweh is not going to feed them cover them or take away any of their sorrows and hurts from them, but will slay them.

[13] Therefore thus saith YHWH, Behold, my servants
shall eat, but ye shall be hungry: behold, my servants shall
drink, but ye shall be thirsty: behold, my servants shall
rejoice, but ye shall be ashamed: [14] Behold, my servants shall
sing for joy of heart, but ye shall cry for sorrow of heart, and
shall howl for vexation of spirit. [15] And ye shall leave your
name for a curse unto my chosen: for I YHWH shall slay
thee, and call his servants by another name. (Is 65-13-15)

It is completely evident John the writer of the book of Revelation took a lot of Yeshayahu the prophets words in his heart because this was the place much of the book came from, many of Johns words were quotes from the prophet Yeshayahu, also Dani'el and (Jeremiah / Yirmeyahu). John expounded on the writings for more clarity and insight, all by the direction of YHWH. Keep in mind gad and meni were both mighty ones of the Romans along with Zues, and the son god Iesous which was also referred to as a son of Zeus. They were all about fortune and increase of knowledge as long as it sounded good, They practiced philosophy, mythology, and fables. They were false gods, deceiving spirits, those who were cast down from the heavenly place who forsook their first estate. Those were also spirits that had their followers do witch craft and sorcery, which made them thieves and robbers, as Yahushua spoke of in (John 10:1-8).

All those false spirits are truly the only enemy of mankind, they are the ones that cause man to do evil and wicked things to others. Look back at history the inquisition and the crusades all were in the name of their god. Now when you look back you will see the heathen did not have writings from their gods, only magicians and soothsayers, star gazers. All were lead by false spirits of some sort or another, it was not until they took the scriptures from the Hebrews, then they had writings. Constantine was the one that decreed the catholic religion to be the world religion, he then started to raise up cathedrals, they called their doctrine the (Papacy). Constantine was calling himself a Vicar of Christ, and so was all the other popes, meaning they considered themselves the replacement of Messiah on earth. Which is and was impossible since they were lead by a false deity that is against mankind.

Vicar–(from Latin vicarius, "substitute"), an official acting in some special way for a superior, primarily an ecclesiastical title in the Christian Church. In the Roman Empire as reorganized by Emperor Diocletian (reigned 284-305), the vicarius was an important official, and the title remained in use for secular officials in the Middle Ages. In the Roman Catholic Church, "vicar of Christ" became the special designation of the popes starting in the 8th century, and eventually it replaced the older title of "vicar of St. Peter." (Source = Encyclopedia Britannica) Why am I showing this to you? Because these are some of who YHWH was referring to.

Remember Roman Catholicism is the beginning of all the tree of Christianity, every denomination and branch is of that tree. The Catholics are those who use YHWH's word but have changed it to keep their ways alive. Mormons also use the scriptures and have doctrines all based on the same King James Version, Scriptures. Jehovah witnesses use the scriptures of YHWH, also based upon the King James Version, although they had made many changes to their scriptures and is no longer the KJV but the Jehovah witness version. Now it is rational for me to say each of these different groups believe whole heartedly upon the scriptures they read, of their denomination.

The Jehovah witnesses beginning–The group emerged from the Bible Student movement founded in the late 1870s by Charles Taze Russel with the formation of Zions Watchtower tract society—with significant organizational and doctrinal changes under the leadership of Joseph F Rutherford The name Jehovah's witnesses, based on Isaiah 43:10–12, was adopted in 1931 to distinguish themselves from other Bible Student groups and symbolize a break with the legacy of Russell's traditions. (source Wikepedia)

Word origin and history of Mormon 1830, coined by religion founder Joseph Smith (1805-1844) in Seneca

County, N.Y., in allusion to Mormon, supposed prophet and author of "The Book of Mormon," explained by Smith as meaning more mon, from Eng. more + Egyptian mon "good." (Source Dictionary.com)

Mormon started by Joseph Smith in the early 1830's. Joseph Smith wrote a book called the Book of Mormons which explains their doctrinal beliefs and by laws. (Source Wikipedia)

All of these denominations of believers were at one time or another considered Christian by belief, and different by doctrine and belief. They all started of with the KJV scriptures and all have different doctrines. All of them have their day of worship on Sunday the first day. Most all of these denominations keep Christmas, Easter, thanksgiving, Ect, except Jehovah witnesses they do not keep those days. I say search out the origin of those holiday's it will blow your mind where they started from, and you will even see the truth about the Catholic religion making them apart of the Holy feast of YHWH, like passover, then feast of Tabernacles. The world keeps halloween or what some call harvest parties. None the less the true Holy Gatherings of YHWH are not kept by the masses of Christians or Jehovah witnesses or the Mormans. Now some made changes according to their findings and beliefs of the scriptures. They formed their own group of believers, the same with many other Christian groups or denominations. Then there are the Muslims which have many different secs of believers and ways. The reason why I am saying these things is as a warning to those who can see the real way and truth, to make the changes needed for your eternal walk with the Father Yah and Yahushua the Messiah. Because many believers are white washed into believing everything is going to be so wonderful in the heavens after they pass on from here. So I show you this bit of scripture to help you realize what needs to be done and what you can do to make it happen so you will have a wonderful eternal home instead of hardship and desperation.

[1] Open thy doors, O Lebanon, that the fire may devour
thy cedars. [2] Howl, fir tree; for the cedar is fallen; because
the mighty are spoiled: howl, O ye oaks of Bashan; for the
forest of the vintage is come down. [3] There is a voice of
the howling of the shepherds; for their glory is spoiled: a
voice of the roaring of young lions; for the pride of Jordan
is spoiled.[4] Thus saith Yahweh my Elohim; Feed the flock
of the slaughter; [5] Whose possessors slay them, and hold
themselves not guilty: and they that sell them say, Blessed
be YHWH; for I am rich: and their own shepherds pity
them not. [6] For I will no more pity the inhabitants of the
land, saith YHWH: but, lo, I will deliver the men every one
into his neighbour's hand, and into the hand of his king: and
they shall smite the land, and out of their hand I will not
deliver them. [7] And I will feed the flock of slaughter, even
you, O poor of the flock. And I took unto me two staves;
the one I called Beauty, and the other I called Bands; and I

fed the flock. [8] Three shepherds also I cut off in one month; and my soul loathed them, and their soul also abhorred me. [9] Then said I, I will not feed you: that dieth, let it die; and that that is to be cut off, let it be cut off; and let the rest eat every one the flesh of another [10] And I took my staff, even Beauty, and cut it asunder, that I might break my covenant which I had made with all the people. [11] And it was broken in that day: and so the poor of the flock that waited upon me knew that it was the word of YHWH. (Zech 11:1-11)

This word was meant for those in the future, just before the eternal paradise. That was not meant for the temporal, when that time comes they will be rejected by YHWH because they have rejected Him on this earth. That means all those following false gods or deceiving spirits will be turned away. Those who know His scriptures but do not follow His, way, but another. Do you think all these people will be getting into the new heavens and the new earth and then praising other mighty ones, and not YHWH? All those other spirits will be done away with and there will not be any other, only Yah the Father and Yahushua the Son. Those of us that are His will be as angles of YHWH in Yahushua, who kept His word His name and did as His word commanded. Many have His word and all have their doctrines of His word, but do they honor YHWH or another spirit? Do they honor Yahushua or another spirit? What about those who believe on YHWH but not Yahushua? We know Yahushua is the beginning of the renewed covenant of YHWH, because Yahushua was the completion of Torah, not the end, but the goal of the torah.

[4] For Messiah is the goal of the (law / Torah) for righteousness to every one that believeth. (Rom 10:4)

Today's religions teach disobedience to the Torah, not realizing the scripture writings from Matthew to Revelation is all about the Torah completion. Only by the Spirit of Yahushua the Messiah is it possible to truly see this wonderful revelation.

Yahushua said He came not to destroy the law but fulfill, that word is the same as to complete or to be the completion of said work. Those ministers who teach the law no longer applies to them, cannot justify that statement because that can only be possible when they are in the lake of fire and brimstone, or the second death! Because the Torah is the future for all who are YHWH's. Righteous instruction, and moral truth, a right spirit in us is through Yahushua. Lawlessness has no place within YHWH's kingdom, nor does the spirit of wickedness. The spirit that disregards (Torah or law) is the same as lawless. That is why the other spirit teaches away from Torah because the end is clear, without YHWH there is no life eternal. As I have said the only true enemy of mankind is the spirits of wickedness and deception, the false spirit is such a spirit. That spirit blinds the eyes of them who are lead by it, to be lawless and unaware of the prophetic truth of YHWH's word. That same spirit tells you the Old Testament does not apply to you any more. I always say to know where you are going you must first know where you came from, the past is relevant to the future because of this tabernacle called our body. Those in false doctrine and religions are of the other spirit the false spirit. Now ultimately you would have to ask who is the false spirit? How do I know if I'm in the false spirit or not? Does your doctrine line up with the scriptures? Is your denomination keeping the word as YHWH said or as man dictates? If you check the scriptures you will see Paul keep YHWH's word and (Torah or Laws) he kept the Sabbath and the feasts of YHWH, as did Yahushua the Messiah. So why do all those religions keep Sunday? Constantine proclaimed them as the world wide religious rules, the Roman leader, said any one keeping the feasts and Sabbaths of the YHWH would be put to death. How important it is to be following the Fathers word, not mans.

24 Therefore as the fire devoureth the stubble, and the flame consumeth the chaff, so their root shall be as rottenness, and their blossom shall go up as dust: because they have cast away the law of YHWH of hosts, and despised the word of the Holy One of Yisrael. (Isa 5:24).

13 Thou art wearied in the multitude of thy counsels. Let now the astrologers the stargazers, the monthly prognosticators, stand up, and save thee from these things
that shall come upon thee. 14 Behold, they shall be as stubble;
the fire shall burn them; they shall not deliver themselves from the power of the flame: there shall not be a coal to

warm at, nor fire to sit before it. [15] Thus shall they be unto thee with whom thou hast laboured, even thy merchants, from thy youth: they shall wander every one to his quarter; none shall save thee.(Isa 47:14)

What about the ministers that say the law no longer applies to us yet they collects tithes from those in the group. Is that not in the (Torah or Law)? Why then is it ok to take tithes when it is in the Torah? And not in the so called New Testament writings. That is a double standard, one that benefits those in the clergy. It is important the scriptures are to be upheld by those who are His, and as I explained before, no you do not stone anyone anymore, the laws of the land are to be obeyed. Now realize all those things are going to come to pass like it or not! YHWH is the eternal all in all and none can out think, out smart, out do, out give, Him nor can anyone take Him out of the place of being the creator and King of all that is was and ever will be. The scriptures clearly say it does not matter if you are Jew or gentile, all who are in Yahushua the Messiah are heirs according to the promise as a seed of Abraham. Faith and obedience to His word is the key to life eternal for us all.

[19] Circumcision is nothing, and uncircumcision is nothing, but the keeping of the commandments of YHWH. (1Cor 7:19)

[13] For this cause also thank we YHWH without ceasing, because, when ye received the word of YHWH which ye heard of us, ye received it not as the word of men, but

as it is in truth, the word of YHWH, which effectually worketh also in you that believe. [14] For ye, brethren, became followers of the assemblies of YHWH which in Yudaea are in Messiah Yahushua : for ye also have suffered like things of your own countrymen, even as they have of the Jews: [15] Who both killed the Messiah Yahushua, and their own prophets, and have persecuted us and they please not YHWH, and are contrary to all men: [16] Forbidding us to speak to the Gentiles that they might be saved, to fill up their sins alway: for the wrath is come upon them to the uttermost. (1Thes 2:13-16)

This is a harsh word from Shaul who said this about the followers of YHWH that did not believe Messiah had already come, because they were blinded to YHWH's Yahushua, and unable to see this truth, and only He knows why? Now Yahushua did come and fulfill the word YHWH spoke through the prophets about His only begotten Son Yahushua the Messiah. So from that day until the end all must become followers of Yahushua and become His anointed to have life eternal. The book of Romans Chpt, 11 says the remnant shall be saved, which His word is true but, He will quicken those so they can see and fully believe here on this earth. Because He said those who reject the Son have not the Father.

[20] But ye have an unction from the Holy One, and ye know all things. [21] I have not written unto you because ye know not the truth, but because ye know it, and that no

lie is of the truth. [22] Who is a liar but he that denieth that Yahushua is the Messiah? He is anti-Messiah, that denieth the Father and the Son. [23] Whosoever denieth the Son, the same hath not the Father: (but) he that acknowledgeth the Son hath the Father also. [24] Let that therefore abide in you, which ye have heard from the beginning. If that which ye have heard from the beginning shall remain in you, ye also shall continue in the Son, and in the Father. [25] And this is the promise that he hath promised us, even eternal life. (1John 2:20-25)

The old saying goes there is more than one way to skin a cat! Satan has deceived the masses for many centuries, false religion is one of his most powerful tools! Many are fooled but once the lie is exposed and brought to light then defused he no longer has power over the masses. This is why the truth is so important, satan knows how to make people be their own worst enemy, he knows the scriptures, and deceives many by them,

The Old and New Testaments, whether you are young or old, satan does not care, to him you are an enemy to his being. When you become what the Father has called you to be, you are then a threat and detriment to satan's ways. Replenish the earth then in time the heavenly hosts will become restored. That is why satan tries to destroy man before they get to know truth, and when they start learning the truth he deceives many into thinking wrong teachings, by his twisting of the word, just like he did with Eve. The true believer should know not to listen to the voices of darkness, some can be deceived, His word gives you the victory over satans deceptions. One reason why the deception can be so strong against many is unknown sin, or doing false worship, not following the word of YHWH, but mans ways. When you sin and continue in it, you become given over to that thing and it rules over you! Controls you! Eventually you can become blinded to any thing else but that rule, well satan is the one doing all those things to the masses, like it or not. He hates mankind and is marked for death, without forgiveness or mercy. False worship and idolatry is all his working, to turn mankind away from YHWH the Father. Remember sin is an open door to his realm, and he is the enemy of all mankind.

[25] In meekness instructing those that oppose themselves;
if YHWH peradventure will give them repentance to
the acknowledging of the truth; [26] that they may recover
themselves out of the snare of the devil, who are taken
captive by him at his will. (2Tim 2:25-26).

That explains much of what I said, but the depths of those deceptions is almost unfathomable, and even hard to except for those who know not the truth. Salvation is a gift from YHWH through His Son Yahushua the Messiah, gift means it is given, you do not have to buy it and cannot. The gift is through the Son Yahushua the Anointed or Messiah and only by His spirit can any man live. Remember

Yahushua said salvation is of the Jews! And by YHWH's design, not mans.

[27] For as many of you as have been baptized into Yahushua have put on Yahushua. [28] There is neither Jew nor Greek, there is neither bond nor free, there is neither male nor female: for ye are all one in Messiah Yahushua. [29] And if ye be Messiah's, then are ye Abraham's seed, and heirs according to the promise. (Gal 3:27-29)

I also should remind you the book of Galatians, does not prove the taking away of the Torah but shows the facts of the matter concerning those in the circumcision, who were turning many away because of the (Law of circumcision)

[30] Seeing it is one Elohim, which shall justify the circumcision by faith, and uncircumcision through faith. [31] Do we then make void the law through faith? YHWH forbid: yea, we establish the law. (Rom 3:30-31)

[1] Stand fast therefore in the liberty wherewith Messiah hath made us free, and be not entangled again with the yoke of bondage. [2] Behold, I Paul say unto you, that if ye be circumcised, Messiah shall profit you nothing. [3] For I testify again to every man that is circumcised, that he is a debtor to do the whole law. [4] Messiah is become of no effect unto you, whosoever of you are justified by the law; ye are fallen from grace. [5] For we through the Spirit wait for the hope of righteousness by faith. [6] For in Yahushua the Messiah neither circumcision availeth any thing, nor uncircumcision; but faith which worketh by love. (Gal 5:1-6)

Yahushua the Messiah took away the ordinances of ritualized works for Salvation, no longer did a man have to slaughter any beast for forgiveness of sins, or become circumcised to keep the covenant of YHWH because those things were a shadow of the Messiah's coming.

1 For the law having a shadow of good things to come, and not the very image of the things, can never with those sacrifices which they offered year by year continually make the comers thereunto perfect. 2 For then would they not have ceased to be offered? Because that the worshippers once purged should have had no more conscience of sins. 3 But in those sacrifices there is a remembrance again made of sins every year. 4 For it is not possible that the blood of bulls and of goats should take away sins. 5 Wherefore when he cometh into the world, he saith, Sacrifice and offering thou wouldest not, but a body hast thou prepared me: 6 In burnt offerings and sacrifices for sin thou hast had no pleasure. 7 Then said I, Lo, I come (in the volume of the book it is written of me,) to do thy will, O YHWH. 8 Above when he said, Sacrifice and offering and burnt offerings and offering for sin thou wouldest not, neither hadst pleasure therein; which are offered by the (law / Torah); 9 Then said he, Lo, I come to do thy will, O YHWH. He taketh away the first, that he may establish the second. 10 By the which will we are sanctified through the offering of the body of Yahushua the Messiah once for all. 11 And every priest standeth daily ministering and offering oftentimes the same sacrifices,

which can never take away sins: [12] But this man, after he had offered one sacrifice for sins for ever, sat down on the right hand of YHWH; [13] From henceforth expecting till his enemies be made his footstool. [14] For by one offering he hath perfected for ever them that are sanctified.

[15] Where of the Holy Spirit also is a witness to us: for after that he had said before,

[16] This is the covenant that I will make with them after those days, saith YHWH, I will put my laws into their hearts, and in their minds will I write them; [17] And their sins and iniquities will I remember no more. (Heb 10:1-17) from (Jer 32:31-33)

When He fulfilled the word and the Torah, this was the out come, the spirit of man could then become cleansed by the perfect spirit of Yahushua. We then are circumcised in heart, which is why we must call upon His name, confess Him and be baptized into the renewed Holy Spirit of life, Yahushua. Then ridding ourselves of the old spirit likeness of the deceiver satan who is also the spirit leader of false gods. Again I will bring to your attention these words:

[30] Seeing it is one Elohim, which shall justify the circumcision by faith, and uncircu-mcision through faith. [31] Do we then make void the law through faith? YHWH forbid: yea, we establish the law. (Rom 3:30-31).

What does it mean to establish the Law? To be obedient to the scriptures as they were written, the intent is to instruct us in the righteous teachings of YHWH. And for us to do the Fathers will which is (Torah also known as Law). If you remember the newer writings many call the New Testament was not written, so what Paul was teaching from and speaking of was the Torah, Law of YHWH! Sha'ul wrote the biggest part of the epistle because He was an apostle, one who was called to evangelize the heathen and start Assemblies in the name of Yahushua the Messiah! Giving praise unto the Father YHWH in the name of the beloved Son Yahushua the Messiah! When you become baptized into the real name of Yahushua the spirit teaches you truth, truth that before was not seen by the other spirits of religiosity or the other spirit. That is why I mentioned learning curve earlier, His spirit compels you to keep His word and His Sabbath, and Feasts! Which former Popes had made other men stop doing, Constantine was that pope! The real reason was they won the war, the Romans, so they made things go their way, Israel was captive by this people of many gods, and why? I believe it was because of idolatry, and YHWH's wrath was kindled against them for sacrificing their own children to Molech like the heathen nations had been doing. YHWH does not take kindly to those ways, He said not to do it, and that was in His Torah.

21 And thou shalt not let any of thy seed pass through the fire to Molech, neither shalt thou profane the name of thy Elohim: I am YHWH.(Lev 18:21)

YHWH is a jealous Elohim, He said it and has proven that statement time and time again. What it means to sacrifice to Molech was the worst form of adulterous idolatry there is, in the eyes of YHWH the Father. But what does it truly mean to be saved. The realization of YHWH making a way for us to escape His wrath and the second death is an awesome thing. But what of those who are completely deceived into thinking all ways lead to heaven? And none will perish. Do you know it says YHWH will weed out those that transgress His directions? This is why He gave us His word, so we can know those things we should do, and not do, in our becoming sons of YHWH. Because the circumcision of our hearts is only a beginning toward eternal life, and walking as YHWH wants for us. Please do not get me wrong YHWH is very merciful and His loving kindness and tender mercies for us is awesome. Because He is LOVE! He is a friend to us who love Him! Because Yahushua the Messiah has given us favor with Him to become sons of YHWH. On the other hand almost every religious group on this earth truly thinks they are right in their religious ways. YHWH gave His word so we could know what to do, but what about those who do not do like His word said? Many religions practice self righteousness and enlightenment. Some practice worship of animals and believe in reincarnation, and what about jehhadist belief of murdering others for their heavenly blessings, we know the scriptures is against those kind of practices. All these people truly believe they will have their reward in a heavenly place, or some kind of equivalent. But it is clearly known by those who follow YHWH it is the word of YHWH that will judge all peoples in the great day, the day of judgment.

15 For, behold, YHWH will come with fire, and with his chariots like a whirlwind, to render his anger with fury, and his rebuke with flames of fire. 16 For by fire and by his sword will YHWH plead with all flesh: and the slain of YHWH shall be many. 17 They that sanctify themselves, and purify themselves in the gardens behind one tree in the midst, eating swine's flesh, and the abomination, and the mouse, shall be consumed together, saith YHWH.(Isa 66:15-17)

22 For as the new heavens and the new earth, which I will make, shall remain before me, saith YHWH of Hosts, so shall your seed and your name remain. 23 And it shall come to pass, that from one new moon to another, and from one Sabbath to another, shall all flesh come to worship before me, saith YHWH. 24 And they shall go forth, and look upon the carcases of the men that have transgressed against me: for their worm shall not die, neither shall their fire be quenched; and they shall be an abhorring unto all flesh.

(Isa 66:22-24)

Who are those that have transgressed? Those who rejected Him and His son by their real names. May be those who completely disregard the son Yahushua His Messiah, or what about those in the other spirit, which is the anti-Messiah spirit. Perhaps it is just them who do not believe He exists? Those who deny His presence in this earth. Them that are lawless committing sin against mankind always doing against YHWH's word of truth. I have talked to some people who believe everyone will live forever eternal, that is not the actual truth. Every one from this earth will live once again but not all will live eternal because those who chose the ways of wickedness will die eternal, that is a big difference and far cry from life. YHWH will repay them to their face that hate him, because vengeance is His and His alone! When a man sins against another man he does not sin against man but YHWH and he repays them that are evil. John said how can you love the Father whom you cannot see, if you cannot love your brother, whom you can see. If you cannot love your fellow man, than how can you love YHWH? I do know then in the eternal place the Torah will be upheld, those who are against YHWH will not be among those who love Him. Yahushua is one who will judge the quickened and the dead, and realize this He uses the righteous judgment of the word. Every circumstance and situation will be covered by the using of His word, according to the scriptures as Yahushua has taught us by His Spirit. He will completely amaze us who are there with Him, His judgments will be awesome, He will speak the word and it will happen as immediate as He pronounces it. To His throne there is no end, the Son shall reign as the one of all authority, and even now is on the throne as Elohim. Now there is a problem for those who do not believe Yahushua is the Messiah, even though His name is a complete and actual, statement of who Yahushua is! YHWH is Salvation. How much plainer can it be? YHWH put His own Holy Spirit into the womb of a righteous woman and made Himself a body! Made under Law, to complete the Torah, Yahushua the Anointed is that Son of YHWH.

1 For the law having a shadow of good things to come,
and not the very image of the things, can never with those
sacrifices which they offered year by year continually make
the comers thereunto perfect. 2 For then would they not
have ceased to be offered? because that the worshippers
once purged should have had no more conscience of
sins. 3 But in those sacrifices there is a remembrance
again made of sins every year. 4 For it is not possible that
the blood of bulls and of goats should take away sins. 5
Wherefore when he cometh into the world, he saith,
Sacrifice and offering thou wouldest not, but a body
hast thou prepared me: (Heb 10:1-5)

1 YHWH, who at sundry times and in divers manners
spake in time past unto the fathers by the prophets, 2 Hath
in these last days spoken unto us by his Son, whom he hath
appointed heir of all things, by whom also he made the
worlds; 3 Who being the brightness of his glory, and the
express image of his person, and upholding all things by
the word of his power, when he had by himself purged our
sins, sat down on the right hand of the Majesty on highJ
(Heb 1:1-3)

If any man has not the son the Father is not with them neither, that is scriptural, and factual. Because Yahushua overcame all principalities and powers of darkness as a man to set us free from the powers of death. Because man cannot be free if he is in the spirit likeness of death. That is for all mankind of all walks and creeds through out the whole world, Jew and gentile alike there is no exception, YHWH is no respecter of persons. Every person on this earth will have to realize Yahushua is the Son of the Most High YHWH. Then realize He is not just a prophet, same for those still under the Abrahamic covenant with Moses. Because YHWH did send His Yahushua for all people. YHWH even spoke it through Moses.

[18] I will raise them up a Prophet from among their
brethren, like unto thee, and will put my words in his mouth;
and he shall speak unto them all that I shall command
him. [19] And it shall come to pass, that whosoever will not
hearken unto my words which he shall speak in my name, I
will require it of him. (Deu 18:18-19)

Yahushua said I come in my Fathers name, and if you have seen Me, you have seen the Father also! For one to speak in the name of the Father also means, to speak in His authority. Yahushua proved His authority when He spoke healings and mighty works through out the lands. Even some of the Pharisees said no man could do such mighty works unless Elohim be with him.

[4] Being made so much better than the angels, as he hath
by inheritance obtained a more excellent name than they. [5]
For unto which of the angels said he at any time, Thou art
my Son, this day have I begotten thee? And again, I will be
to him a Father, and he shall be to me a Son? [6] And again
when he bringeth in the first begotten into the world, he
saith, And let all the angels of YHWH worship him. [7] And
of the angels he saith, Who maketh his angels spirits, and
his ministers a flame of fire. [8] But unto the Son he saith,
Thy throne, O Elohim, is for ever and ever: a sceptre of
righteousness is the sceptre of thy kingdom. [9] Thou hast
loved righteousness, and hated iniquity; therefore Elohim,
even thy Elohim, hath anointed thee with the oil of gladness
above thy fellows. [10] And, Thou, Master, in the beginning
hast laid the foundation of the earth; and the heavens are
the works of thine hands: [11] They shall perish; but thou
remainest; and they all shall wax old as doth a garment; [12]
And as a vesture shalt thou fold them up, and they shall be
changed: but thou art the same, and thy years shall not fail.
[13] But to which of the angels said he at any time, Sit on my
right hand, until I make thine enemies thy footstool? [14] Are
they not all ministering spirits, sent forth to minister for
them who shall be heirs of salvation? (Heb 1:4-14)

So YHWH has also stated he has changed the covenant
to bring all mankind into His word and way [1] Now of the
things which we have spoken this is the sum: We have such
an high priest, who is set on the right hand of the throne

of the Majesty in the heavens; 2 A minister of the sanctuary
and of the true tabernacle, which YHWH pitched, and not
man. 3 For every high priest is ordained to offer gifts and
sacrifices: wherefore it is of necessity that this man have
somewhat also to offer. 4 For if he were on earth, he should
not be a priest, seeing that there are priests that offer gifts
according to the law / Torah: 5 Who serve unto the example
and shadow of heavenly things, as Moses was admonished
of YHWH when he was about to make the tabernacle: for,
See, saith He, that thou make all things according to the
pattern shewed to thee in the mount. 6 But now hath he
obtained a more_excellent ministry, by how much also he
is the mediator of a better covenant which was established
upon better promises. 7 For if that first covenant had been
faultless, then should no place have been sought for the
second._ 8 For finding fault with them, he saith, Behold, the
days come, saith YHWH, when I will make a new covenant
with the house of Israel and with the house of Judah: 9 Not
according to the covenant that I made with their fathers
in the day when I took them by the hand to lead them out
of the land of Egypt; because they continued not in my
covenant, and I regarded them not, saith YHWH.

10 For this is the covenant that I will make with the
house of Israel after those days, saith YHWH; I will put
my laws into their mind, and write them in their hearts:
and I will be to them a Elohim, and they shall be to
me a people: 11 And they shall not teach every man his

neighbour, and every man his brother, saying, Know YHWH: for all shall know me, from the least to the greatest. [12] For I will be merciful to their unrighteousness, and their sins and their iniquities will I remember no more. [13] In that he saith, A new covenant, he hath made the first old. Now that which decayeth and waxeth old is ready to vanish away. (Heb 8:1-13)

It is a fact these scripture writings have been authenticated and date back to ancient scroll writings and so is fact not made up, no Jewish rabbi can dispute the Torah, has been fulfilled by YHWH by His Yahushua. But the Jewish leaders would not go forth with the good news of Yahushua because of their hard headedness and the facts are they did not believe in Yahushua, they were the ones in charge of the scriptures then. They even thought their words had more authority then YHWH's. The real deal is YHWH did as He said, and even the words Yahushua said ring loudly in our hearts as YHWH's words speaking directly to the hearts and souls of His people. This is because He loves you, and your children who He has blessed. You may not have seen this until now, YHWH has fulfilled His word in you and your children. With the desire of your sight be made true by His beloved Son Yahushua. But every person has a right to search out YHWH's truth and become His and follow Messiah as He teaches them by His Spirit. Make no mistake you that know the Torah have an advantage of knowing the Fathers will but are disadvantaged if you have the spiritual likeness of Moses and cannot become complete as YHWH desires without Messiah Yahushua. And so many others in the worldly religion of Christianity are at an advantage because they realize the Messiah has come, but they also are at a disadvantage because they disregard the Fathers will over mans. So it remains to be seen by those in their perspective religions to search out His real truth and become a follower of the scriptures and not a follower of men. Moses did not enter in! YHWH stopped him before the crossing over the Jordan for a reason. Instead YHWH told Moses to lay hands on Hosea son of Nunn and said speak as I tell you, and so what did Mosheh call Him Yehoshua son of Nunn, YHWH told you then in the scriptures the Name of the Messiah was going to be Yahushua and He did as YHWH said, then all that did not die in the wilderness, entered in as YHWH spoke to them. That truly was a message for the generations to come, and for every religion that uses YHWH's scriptures for their righteous teaching. That was the shadow of what was to come, why? Because Moses did not have the Spiritual likeness of the Son, he was in the old likeness. But all those who were faithful to YHWH under the old covenant before Messiahs ascension will be brought into the true likeness by Messiah, as the prophets wrote, He will purge the Levite so they can do righteous offerings as in the days of old. It is imperative to salvation for all mankind, ye must have the Son Yahushua as your spirit leader, teacher, Master, the advocate to the Father

YHWH! It is absolute! No exceptions apply to this order made by YHWH Himself. (See- Deu 18:18) I do not think YHWH had to add to His word, especially when it comes to a wife or the treatment of a wife. YHWH said He is not happy when men abuse their wives.

[10] Have we not all one father? hath not one Elohim created us? why do we deal treacherously every man against his brother, by profaning the covenant of our fathers?
[11] Yudah hath dealt treacherously, and an abomination is committed in Israel and in Yerusalem; for Yudah hath profaned the holiness of YHWH which he loved and hath married the daughter of a strange gods. [12] YHWH will cut off the man that doeth this, the master and the scholar, out of the tabernacles of Ya'aqob, and him that offereth an offering unto YHWH of hosts. [13] And this have ye done again, covering the altar of YHWH with tears, with weeping, and with crying out, insomuch that He regardeth not the offering any more, or receiveth it with good will at your hand.
[14] Yet ye say, wherefore? Because YHWH hath been witness between thee and the wife of thy youth, against whom thou hast dealt treacherously: yet is she thy companion, and the wife of thy covenant. [15] And did not he make one? Yet had he the residue of the spirit. And wherefore one? That he might seek a holy seed. Therefore take heed to your spirit, and let none deal treacherously against the wife of his youth.
[16] For YHWH, the Elohim of Israel, saith that he hateth putting away: for one covereth violence with his garment,

saith YHWH of hosts: therefore take heed to your spirit, that ye deal not treacherously. (Mal 2:10-16)

[10] And the man that committeth adultery with another man's wife, even he that committeth adultery with his neighbour's wife, the adulterer and the adulteress shall surely be put to death. (Lev 20:10)

[2] Nevertheless, to avoid fornication, let every man have
his own wife, and let every woman have her own husband. [3]
Let the husband render unto the wife due benevolence: and
likewise also the wife unto the husband. [4] The wife hath not
power of her own body, but the husband: and likewise also
the husband hath not power of his own body, but the wife.
[5] Defraud ye not one the other, except it be with consent
for a time, that ye may give yourselves to fasting and prayer;
and come together again, that Satan tempt you not for your
incontinency.(1Cor 7:2-5)

I do believe this next scripture explains it better than any one could as concerning how a husband should love his wife. Wives should search out the meaning of reverence in the biblical sense.

[25] Husbands, love your wives, even as Messiah also
loved the assembly, and gave himself for it; [26] That he
might sanctify and cleanse it with the washing of water by
the word,

[27] That he might present it to himself a glorious assembly,
not having spot, or wrinkle, or any such thing; but that it
should be holy and without blemish. [28] So ought men to

love their wives as their own bodies. He that loveth his
wife loveth himself. [29] For no man ever yet hated his own
flesh; but nourisheth and cherisheth it, even as Messiah the
assembly: [30] For we are members of his body, of his flesh, and
of his bones. [31] For this cause shall a man leave his father and
mother, and shall be joined unto his wife, and they two shall
be one flesh. [32] This is a great mystery: but I speak concerning
Messiah and the assembly. [33] Nevertheless let every one of
you in particular so love his wife even as himself; and the wife
see that she reverence her husband.(Eph 5:25-33)

What kind of love has Messiah showered upon you men? Unconditional love, the overcoming love, and power of deliverance, and tender mercies. And let us not forget the gift of life, Salvation, eternal life. I will say to all men out there we all should love our wives with unconditional love and forgiveness and shower them with affections of tenderness. You should know you will be heirs together in the eternal home. YHWH does not see one of you without the other! Messiah is able to direct you men into this role of being her true husband man and love of her life, so she will be to you, a virtues wife. One who reverences her husband in true love and awe? You have a duty to your wife to be a protector and spiritual leader of your family. Men if you are not married make sure she is of this same walk, as you are in Messiah Yahushua, so ye are both able to be compatible. If she will not take sound doctrine or reason with you and hear you, consider the consequences.

She may become your worst enemy, the after math could destroy your eternal futures severely. It is important for you to make sure because if she does not revere you, she does not love you, and if she does against you even a little she cannot care of you. When you marry you are one flesh in the spirit, and when apart in your daily routines, without regard for one another you may both become damaged severely. This for both the man and woman, if you lie even about the smallest issue, before you marry it will come back to haunt your lives together. So be very careful and take time to make sure both are in Yahushua and not another spirit of salvation. Women if by chance you have a boyfriend hit you walk away, it will only get worse, and it is better to walk away than suffer permanent brokenness, and baggage all the rest of your life! That is not right nor is it to be tolerated, by either man or woman in the marriage. And remember anyone can say they are a believer, but it is by their fruits ye shall know them, do they walk the walk and keep the word dear in their hearts? Only a time will tell, so do not rush into a marriage or consummation of a relationship without first praying fervently and knowing the answer of your question was answered according to scripture. Some people draw out a marriage plan based on their future desires and economic standing, because there is allot at steak and lives are in the balance, it has more impact when in writing. Remember a marriage is a covenant, just like a contract for the future of your life. But also keep your communications between you and your future spouse open and honest, and it should be a permanent standing rule in the household of your love together, truth as Yahushua has desired of us is a must for a blessed marriage. So husbands love your wives as you would have them love you, in truth and love. Wives remember YHWH made the man the head of the marriage, this is why the word reverence is used in describing the way you should be with your husband, and reverence has a powerful meaning. It is best not to take advantage of one another because life is to short to destroy a good marriage, so be careful work at your marriage and do not give up. A righteous marriage is Yahweh's delight, the scriptures say blessed is the man who finds himself a good wife! But remember to love her with all your love and encourage the positive ways of truth so as to wash her in the water of the word, for that is the will of YHWH for you in your marriage. Paul wrote this in Ephesians to let all men know they are to be the spiritual head and leader of the union, and this is and was the will of YHWH for man to lead his wife and children to truth and holiness of His word. You see love overcomes all things, love is long suffering, love is kind, love is not hurtful and with the love of Yahushua we are able to love unconditionally. Love is not just a word to be used, but an action that is seen much like faith, by their fruits are they known. Think of the depth of real true unconditional love, this is the power to overcome all the works of evil and the grips of satan. Just as anger is a tool used by spiritual darkness, love destroys the evil intentions and power over man. Much like a soft word turns away wrath, so love turns evil away, His word even says overcome evil with good, so know this only love is good. So men are to teach and direct the family in love! To have a perfect balance in your life you must have love and direction in proper order as scripture says there is a time for love and a time for rest a time for all things. This you should keep near and dear to your thoughts, balance is a delight of YHWH, HalleluYah! These things can truly be achieved with Yahushua's help and much prayer and supplication, knowing you are a vessel of truth and the living Tabernacle of the Holy Spirit of YHWH. This is why we are able to accomplish these things spoken of by the Apostle Sha'ul. The depth of His love in us is unfathomable to comprehend for many even when they know Him by His true way and name, because to know the love of Messiah is a blessed revelation to seek from Him in your learning.

As Paul wrote, [17] That Messiah may dwell in your hearts by faith; that ye, being rooted and grounded in love,[18] May be able to comprehend with all saints what is the breadth, and length, and depth, and height;[19] And to know the love of Messiah which passeth knowledge, that ye might be filled with all the fullness of Elohim. (Eph 3:17-19)

Yahushua the Messiah is the spiritual completeness for all mankind for those who believe and walk in the truth. He is our perfect example and good shepherd, His voice is the voice we must learn from in our studies. He is the teacher we are the future heir of salvation.

1 Verily, verily, I say unto you, He that entereth not by the
door into the sheepfold, but climbeth up some other way,
the same is a thief and a robber. 2 But he that entereth in by
the door is the shepherd of the sheep. 3 To him the porter
openeth; and the sheep hear his voice: and he calleth his
own sheep by name, and leadeth them out. 4 And when he
putteth forth his own sheep, he goeth before them, and the
sheep follow him: for they know his voice. 5 And a stranger
will they not follow, but will flee from him: for they know
not the voice of strangers.(John 10:1-5)

A stranger they will not hear, think about that, in order for you to hear His voice you must know Him. If you are hearing another voice, like a familiar spirit or anti- Messiah spirit and following that voice, then you will not hear the Master Yahushua until the Day of Judgment. That is why Yahushua said this.

18 A good tree cannot bring forth evil fruit, neither can
a corrupt tree bring forth good fruit. 19 Every tree that
bringeth not forth good fruit is hewn down, and cast into
the fire. 20 Wherefore by their fruits ye shall know them.
21 Not every one that saith unto me, Master, Master, shall
enter into the kingdom of heaven; but he that doeth the
will of my Father which is in heaven. 22 Many will say to
me in that day, Master, Master, have we not prophesied in
thy name? and in thy name have cast out devils? and in

thy name done many wonderful works? [23] And then will I profess unto them, I never knew you: depart from me, ye that work iniquity.(Mat 7:18-23)

Those did not know Him but another mighty one, they had been taught by a spirit that was not Yahushua the Messiah, but another. That is why He said I never knew you! Because of false religion and the being misled by the ant-Messiah spirit. That spirit is contrary to Yahushua and the Father YHWH, and does not teach the will of the Father YHWH but the will of main stream easy beliefs. The kind of belief that picks and chooses what is to be used out of the scriptures, for their doctrine and teachings, which is contrary to Messiah's true reason for His ascension into the heavenly place. He came to fulfill not destroy, to restore that which was lost. What was lost? The right spirit of man when Adam and Eve fell.

[13] (For until the law sin was in the world: but sin is not imputed when there is no law.

[14] Nevertheless death reigned from Adam to Moses, even over them that had not sinned after the similitude of Adam's transgression, who is the figure of him that was to come. (Rom 5:13-14)

That is why all the temple works were a shadow of the future things to come. The sacrifices are all done away with because Yahushua fulfilled the purpose he was sent here for. He restored the true spirit of righteousness in those who believe in Him and seek the truth in the Father YHWH.

The most important thing to be realized is Yahushua is our completion, the author and finisher of our souls and faith. Remember Yahushua is the resurrection and the life, all who would believe on Him shall not see death but have everlasting life. In all our searching we should search and ask for the truth, the real way, the path that leads us to the real and true Elohim and Father YHWH. In the past I heard a few ministers say this walk was to hard for people, and none would make it to the true way. I say "Hogwash!" Man was made to conquer in the mighty name of Him that is truth, Yahushua the Messiah. This is also the reason they pick and choose the scriptures that are taught to the groups of followers, and why many say the Old Testament is past away and no longer applies to the new covenant, but it does apply, completely. Even the word Torah applies to every believer on this earth who seeks truth, because Yahushua did not abolish the Torah but fulfilled it so we could enter into the place of holiness and righteousness of YHWH! The goal is for us all to become sons of YHWH cleansed and like Messiah Yahushua,

4 For Messiah is the (goal / end) of the (law / Torah) for righteousness to every one that believeth. (Rom 10:4)

The word end means goal, the end purpose not the end of, but rather a beginning of son ship with the Father in Yahushua the Messiah. So why is it so many say the way is to hard to keep? Because of false religion! So many are doing what everyone else is doing, just because we have always done it that way. It is the will of the Father that all would be saved and come unto the knowledge of the truth. We are only here for one reason to replenish the angelic host of YHWH! When that is done all else will be tossed into the lake of fire where the worm dieth not and the fire be not quenched. The teaching of the 144,000 is not what many seem to think it is, that is not the number of all who will be saved, because of the Fathers will that all be saved. Seek this truth brethren it is a wonderful thing to see and learn. But for the 144,000 they are those who will serve Messiah night and day, and will reign with him in the thousand year millennium. That means they will minister night and day in the thousand years to help all those who had been deceived who believe in the Messiah and the Father YHWH, false ministers not included they already made their decision whom they are serving and will be judged in the second resurrection according to all their works. YHWH said do not steal, and do not covet another mans anything. So the 144,000 are going to minister Yahushua the Messiah and the Father more perfectly than ever before, and the Torah will go out to the masses and take hold of their hearts. This will bring them into a better understanding of truth, and the ways of the Master. This will be done in peace, because satan will be locked up and not able to hinder anyone on the earth until his time to deceive, when the thousand years is up. That is why the 144,00 are ministering night and day there purpose is to teach the masses of believers so they will not be deceive and follow satan. Because all those who are deceived after that day will be destroyed by fire from heaven.

1 And I looked, and, lo, a Lamb stood on the mount
Sion, and with him an hundred forty and four thousand,
having his Father's name written in their foreheads. 2 And
I heard a voice from heaven, as the voice of many waters,
and as the voice of a great thunder: and I heard the voice
of harpers harping with their harps: 3 And they sung as
it were a new song before the throne, and before the four
beasts, and the elders: and no man could learn that song
but the hundred and forty and four thousand, which were
redeemed from the earth. 4 These are they which were not
defiled with women; for they are virgins. These are they
which follow the Lamb whithersoever he goeth. These
were redeemed from among men, being the first fruits unto
YHWH and to the Lamb. 5 And in their mouth was found
no guile: for they are without fault before the throne of
YHWH. (Rev 14:1-5)

1 And I saw an angel come down from heaven, having
the key of the bottomless pit and a great chain in his hand.
2 And he laid hold on the dragon, that old serpent, which is
the Devil, and Satan, and bound him a thousand years, 3 And
cast him into the bottomless pit, and shut him up, and set a
seal upon him, that he should deceive the nations no more,
till the thousand years should be fulfilled: and after that he
must be loosed a little season. 4 And I saw thrones, and they
sat upon them, and judgment was given unto them: and I

saw the souls of them that were beheaded for the witness of Yahushua, and for the word of YHWH, and which had not worshipped the beast, neither his image, neither had received his mark upon their foreheads, or in their hands; and they lived and reigned with Yahushua a thousand years.
[5] But the rest of the dead lived not again until the thousand
years were finished. This is the first resurrection. [6] Blessed
and holy is he that hath part in the first resurrection: on such the second death hath no power, but they shall be priests of YHWH and of Messiah Yahushua, and shall reign with him a thousand years.

[7] And when the thousand years are expired, Satan shall be loosed out of his prison,

[8] And shall go out to deceive the nations which are in the four quarters of the earth, Gog and Magog, to gather them together to battle: the number of whom is as the
sand of the sea. [9] And they went up on the breadth of the
earth, and compassed the camp of the saints about, and the beloved city: and fire came down from YHWH out of
heaven, and devoured them. [10] And the devil that deceived
them was cast into the lake of fire and brimstone, where the beast and the false prophet are, and shall be tormented day and night for ever and ever. (Rev 20:1-10)

1And after these things I saw four angels standing on the four corners of the earth, holding the four winds of the earth, that the wind should not blow on the earth, nor on the sea, nor on any tree.2 And I saw another angel ascending

from the east, having the seal of the living God: and he
cried with a loud voice to the four angels, to whom it was
given to hurt the earth and the sea, 3 Saying, Hurt not the
earth, neither the sea, nor the trees, till we have sealed the
servants of our Elohim in their foreheads. 4 And I heard the
number of them which were sealed:_and there were sealed
an hundred and forty and four thousand of all the tribes
of the children of Israel. 5 Of the tribe of Juda were sealed
twelve thousand. Of the tribe of Reuben were sealed twelve
thousand. Of the tribe of Gad were sealed twelve thousand.
6 Of the tribe of Aser were sealed twelve thousand. Of the
tribe of Nepthali were sealed twelve thousand. Of the tribe
of Manasses were sealed twelve thousand. 7 Of the tribe
of Simeon were sealed twelve thousand. Of the tribe of
Levi were sealed twelve thousand. Of the tribe of Issachar
were sealed twelve thousand. 8 Of the tribe of Zabulon
were sealed twelve thousand. Of the tribe of Joseph were
sealed twelve thousand. Of the tribe of Benjamin were
sealed twelve thousand. 9 After this I beheld, and, lo, a great
multitude, which no man could number, of all nations,
and kindreds, and people, and tongues, stood before the
throne, and before the Lamb, clothed with white robes, and
palms in their hands; 10 And cried with a loud voice, saying,
Salvation to our Elohim which sitteth upon the throne, and
unto the Lamb. 11 And all the angels stood round about the
throne, and about the elders and the four beasts, and fell
before the throne on their faces, and worshipped YHWH,

[12] Saying, Amen: Blessing, and glory, and wisdom, and thanksgiving, and honour, and power, and might, be unto YHWH for ever and ever. Amen. (Rev 7:1-12)

In the wake of truth is deliverance and spiritual increase, this we all need to realize, is YHWH's desire for us all. As we become more knowledgeable we become more complete in Messiah's spiritual likeness. That is His plan for us all to be sons of YHWH heirs like Messiah, according to the seed of Abraham. The power of YHWH's word is the spiritual manifestation of His changing our inner man, to the likeness of His own son Yahushua this is why we are to become filled with His word. Yahushua said the words He speaks are life.

[62] What and if ye shall see the Son of man ascend up
where he was before? [63] It is the spirit that quickeneth; the
flesh profiteth nothing: the words that I speak unto you,
they are spirit, and they are life. [64] But there are some of you
that believe not. For Yahushua knew from the beginning
who they were that believed not, and who should betray
him. [65] And he said, Therefore said I unto you, that no man
can come unto me, except it were given unto him of my
Father. (John 6:62-65)

The life is formed in those who learn and study to show thy self approved unto YHWH. Sha'ul said it well in the epistle to the Galatians.

[19] My little children, of whom I travail in birth again until Messiah be formed in you, (Gal 4:19)

Then it must be realized the Messiah is the spirit of favor and truth for us who seek the true way and the spiritual manifestation of His likeness for our being. This hunger for His knowledge needs to be fed, for our enlightenment and revelational insight. That is how we learn the truth, by His revealing the mysteries of His knowledge to us.

4 And this I say, lest any man should beguile you with
enticing words. 5 For though I be absent in the flesh, yet am
I with you in the spirit, joying and beholding your order,
and the stedfastness of your faith in Yahushua. 6 As ye have
therefore received Yahushua the Master, so walk ye in him:
7 Rooted and built up in him, and stablished in the faith, as
ye have been taught, abounding therein with thanksgiving. 8
Beware lest any man spoil you through philosophy and vain
deceit, after the tradition of men, after the rudiments of the
world, and not after Yahushua. 9 For in him dwelleth all the
fulness of YHWH the Father bodily. 10 And ye are complete
in him, which is the head of all principality and power: 11 In
whom also ye are circumcised with the circumcision made
without hands, in putting off the body of the sins of the
flesh by the circumcision of Messiah: (Col 2:4-11)

It is a good thing to be like Messiah and walk in Him as we are to put off the ways of the world and be a light of life to others. Because of the circumcision of our spirit man, we are going to become completely renewed. A righteous and holy spiritual being in Messiah. Remember we are to become as angels of YHWH.

[23] The same day came to him the Sadducees, which say that there is no resurrection, and asked him, [24] Saying, Master, Moses said, If a man die, having no children, his brother shall marry his wife, and raise up seed unto his brother. [25] Now there were with us seven brethren: and the first, when he had married a wife, deceased, and, having no issue, left his wife unto his brother: [26] Likewise the second also, and the third, unto the seventh[27] And last of all the woman died also. [28] Therefore in the resurrection whose wife shall she be of the seven? for they all had her. [29] Yahushua answered and said unto them, Ye do err, not knowing the scriptures, nor the power of YHWH. [30] For in the resurrection they neither marry, nor are given in marriage, but are as the angels of YHWH in heaven. [31] But as touching the resurrection of the dead, have ye not read that which was spoken unto you by YHWH, saying, [32] I am the Elohim of Abraham, and the Elohim of Isaac, and the Elohim of Jacob? YHWH is not the Elohim of the dead, but of the living. [33] And when the multitude heard this, they were astonished at his doctrine. (Mat 22:23-33)

Why were those people astonished at the doctrine of Yahushua? Because it was not what they had been used to hearing, Yahushua had the real truth, the kind of truth that sets people free from religious bondage. Many in that day used religion as a control mechanism- to keep people in subjection. So all the people were astonished because Yahushua was speaking a truth that enlightened and did not control but reproved the Sadducees, and religious leaders of that day. Yahushua did that by using the scriptures and not His own words, because the religious leaders could not argue with the truth in scripture, and because He shut the mouths of the religious leaders of that day.

[6] And he said unto me, these sayings are faithful and
true: and Yahweh Elohim of the holy prophets sent his
angel to shew unto his servants the things which must
shortly be done. [7] Behold, I come quickly: blessed is he that
keepeth the sayings of the prophecy of this book. [8] And I
John saw these things, and heard them. And when I had
heard and seen, I fell down to worship before the feet of
the angel which shewed me these things. [9] Then saith he
unto me, See thou do it not: for I am thy fellow servant, and
of thy brethren the prophets, and of them which keep the
sayings of this book: worship Yahweh. (Rev 22:6-9)

This is a look at some revelations of His words spoken by Him to all people who hear, see, and believe He is. He came and conquered all the false spirits by His word. By His example of speech from the good news we see the scriptures is what pushes back the evil working against man. This is called the power of the word! it convicts, condemns, corrects, enlightens, and fixes broken spirits, and makes one glad with joyful happiness. The word is the only thing powerful enough to break through the darkness of mans soul and free him from the darkness working against mankind. Because the enlightenment of the spirit is freedom and liberty from the spirit of death. I know YHWH allows things for our cleansing, sometimes evil prevails till a certain time, to set free a person of His choosing, to open his eyes or bring them into life. But either way it is wonderful to know YHWH never gives up on those who are His, HalleluYah! Just like the things I'm writing here they are to help all who read this to see the truth, and be set free from lies and deceptions, not because I say so but because by them you will seek the real true way and find it. This is the will of YHWH for all who seek, because He does love us and wants us all to be with Him in the eternal home and to know His true Son and beloved Yahushua the Messiah. YHWH's love is awesome to those of us who know Him, He is freeing you from false religion and lies of the darkness. In His light darkness cannot thrive, it becomes transparent and seen or burns into nothingness. YHWH is saving all of us from His wrath! How hard it is for Him to destroy His creation of whom He has showered much favor upon. Since we know we are replenishing the earth, this is not His first rodeo, and perhaps not His last. But we know scripture cannot be broken as Yahushua said, so it will all come to pass as He said it would through the prophets and His apostles.

It is time to know if you feel you are to be a shepherd in Yahushua then shepherd and if a preacher then speak His word to those He sends you to, if you have the calling do not waist the time is drawing nigh. His name is becoming known all over the earth and nothing can stop this from happening. Those false ministers that have taken a pact against the true and real name of the Messiah Yahushua will not win over the will of the Father YHWH. They are the ones who are in the anti- Messiah spirit, changing doctrine and preaching another Messiah. Which tells us all if they are against Yahushua they are also against the true and only creator as well! We must seek the will of the Father YHWH who is in heaven to see His way! Then do not compromise with false teachings of the past, but forge onward into truth. That is the only way to true reckoning of life with Yahushua the Messiah. This is because of His love He bestowed upon man from the beginning, to overcome the powers of darkness and death. I do know if you are truly looking into the things written here, you should have by now realized some truth you may have never seen before. I asure you, it is a true eye opener for all who see the truth after doing all their lives, what they thought was the truth. Then finding out and realizing man has made his own religion and ways of worship, that have nothing to do with the true creator YHWH. Most of the people that come to this realization of truth, go through a pattern of changes- changes that are not easy to deal with. Many search out the facts of this walk I call the true way, because this is what the first believers in Messiah did, they followed as the scriptures say. The book of Acts tells us what the Apostles went through and many of the believers trials. But It does not tell you what happened after the book of Acts or how many millions of people died to share the message with others. The true way was almost totally eradicated by the Roman Catholics, and Constantine. Before the scriptures was translated into English, it was said over five hundred million people had been burned alive, beheaded, buried alive and just run through with a sword or a spear. Because they would not except the sacraments of the Catholic church and it's doctrine, they refused to recognize the popes as Vicars of Messiah, or believe they were their leaders. They were martyrs for their belief in the real truth in Messiah and His way. Why is that? Because they all kept His word to the very last breathe in their bodies. Over and over again the newer writings tell us to establish the Torah, and by the spirit of Messiah in us we can keep Torah. Messiah said we are to become sons and do the will of the Father. Now many of the ministers in today's religions over and over again say the Old Testament or in other words the law or Torah no longer applies to us because we are under a new covenant, which is half truth. Because we that believe in Messiah are under a renewed covenant, that no longer serves the law of animal sacrifice, or the law of circumcision. Because we are the spiritual circumcision of life in Messiah. That is why the book of Galatians was taken out of context, the religious leaders of today's Christian and catholic churches teach from it saying the law and Torah was done away with and no longer applies to us in this day and age. But I asure you if you seek the real truth you will see Paul was speaking to those who regressed because of men preaching of the law of circumcision. Because the Torah or law said the male child must be circumcised on the eighth day, and in the Covenant of Abraham it is a must for Salvation in YHWH, and to be one of His. But because of Messiah Yahushua we are no longer spiritually dead but a spiritually circumcised living man. The argument was only about circumcision of the flesh, not law of the spirit, because there is no law of death for those in Messiah. Remember no man could keep Torah completely until Messiah's Spirit of life was with them. The Ten Commandments are very clear, but so are the other laws spoken in the scriptures.

1 And YHWH spake all these words, saying, 2 I am
YHWH thy Elohim, which have brought thee out of the
land of Egypt, out of the house of bondage 3 Thou shalt
have no other el's before me. 4 Thou shalt not make unto
thee any graven image, or any likeness of any thing that is
in heaven above, or that is in the earth beneath, or that is
in the water under the earth: 5 Thou shalt not bow down
thyself to them, nor serve them: for I YHWH thy Elohim
am a jealous Elohim, visiting the iniquity of the fathers
upon the children unto the third and fourth generation of
them that hate me; 6 And shewing mercy unto thousands
of them that love me, and keep my commandments. 7 Thou
shalt not take the name of YHWH thy Elohim in vain; for
YHWH will not hold him guiltless that taketh his name in

vain. [8] Remember the Sabbath day, to keep it holy. [9] Six days shalt thou labour, and do all thy work: [10] But the seventh day is the Sabbath of YHWH thy Elohim: in it thou shalt not do any work, thou, nor thy son, nor thy daughter, thy manservant, nor thy maidservant, nor thy cattle, nor thy stranger that is within thy gates: [11] For in six days YHWH made heaven and earth, the sea, and all that in them is, and rested the seventh day: wherefore YHWH blessed the Sabbath day, and hallowed it. [12] Honour thy father and thy mother: that thy days may be long upon the land which YHWH thy Elohim giveth thee. [13] Thou shalt not kill. [14] Thou shalt not commit adultery. [15] Thou shalt not steal. [16] Thou shalt not bear false witness against thy neighbour. [17] Thou shalt not covet thy neighbour's house, thou shalt not covet thy neighbour's wife, nor his manservant, nor his maidservant, nor his ox, nor his ass, nor any thing that is thy neighbour's. (Ex 20:1-17)

YHWH made the Sabbath for us to have a day of rest and worship! He said the seventh day He rested and made it Holy, this is the true day of rest and worship unto the real creator YHWH, the one who wrote the bible you read. Israel still keeps the Sabbath of YHWH. And all who are His keep His Sabbath, and His holy days, and not mans.

[1] Thus the heavens and the earth were finished, and all the host of them. [2] And on the seventh day YHWH ended his work which he had made; and he rested on the seventh day from all his work which he had made. [3] And YHWH

blessed the seventh day, and sanctified it: because that in it he had rested from all his work which YHWH created and made.(Gen 2:1-3)

So if you search the scriptures you will see the importance of keeping His Sabbath, because He says you are not His if you do not keep His Sabbath, but another's. Many Pagan holidays and rituals go back to false deities like the goddess Diana and Estara, Molech, and other false gods. These are where the man-made holidays like Christmas, Easter, Halloween, came from. They were all incorporated into play by the Roman Catholic Church. They are all pagan holidays not YHWH's, and these things can be searched out. I have shared with many people in Christianity, Mormonism, Jehovah witnesses, and for some reason many say the same things, the name is not that important or I worship Him on the only day I can or my favorite one he knows my heart. Well if He truly knows your heart then why don't you listen and do it His way and not the man way? He has made it clear in the scriptures He does not fool around when it comes to His plan for us all, and the scriptures covers everything under the sun!

6 My people are destroyed for lack of knowledge: because thou hast rejected knowledge, I will also reject thee, that thou shalt be no priest to me: seeing thou hast forgotten the law of thy Elohim YHWH, I will also forget thy children. (Hose 4:6)

Yea I know, He knows your heart, hmm you think YHWH knew their hearts to, His chosen people that He led by the hand out of the bonds of Egypt! So what did they do to kindle His wrath but worship their own ways. They disregarded His word, His knowledge, His scriptures, and sought after false gods.

1 And now, O ye priests, this commandment is for you.
2 If ye will not hear, and if ye will not lay it to heart, to give
glory unto my name, saith YHWH of hosts, I will even
send a curse upon you, and I will curse your blessings: yea, I
have cursed them already, because ye do not lay it to heart.
3 Behold, I will corrupt your seed, and spread dung upon
your faces, even the dung of your solemn feasts; and one
shall take you away with it. 4 And ye shall know that I have
sent this commandment unto you, that my covenant might
be with Levi, saith YHWH of hosts. 5 My covenant was
with him of life and peace; and I gave them to him for
the fear wherewith he feared me, and was afraid before my
name. 6 The law of truth was in his mouth, and iniquity
was not found in his lips: he walked with me in peace and
equity, and did turn many away from iniquity. 7 For the
priest's lips should keep knowledge, and they should seek
the law at his mouth: for he is the messenger of YHWH of
hosts. 8 But ye are departed out of the way; ye have caused
many to stumble at the law; ye have corrupted the covenant
of Levi, saith YHWH of hosts. 9 Therefore have I also made
you contemptible and base before all the people, according

as ye have not kept my ways, but have been partial in the law.(Mal 2:1-9)

If you are using the scriptures of YHWH that means all the scriptures apply for everyone keeping His word, that applies to all not just the Israeli people. Do you lift up false deities, other spirits, are you committing spiritual adultery against the creator YHWH. If so then you are in need of repentance He will excuse all the times you rejected His real name and His Sons real name, for another one. Because of your realization to His truth and the man-made deception. Because He does not turn a true heart felt repented person away. And it is the truth He does know the heart of man, and has said mans heart is continually evil. So I say reconsider His way and truth before you decide to disregard (Torah / law) He is in the book that he wrote, to love and to guide, to build up, and to tear down, but most of all to save those who are His, and who call upon His name YHWH! It is a fact all who take His word to heart and seek Him find Him.

5 My covenant was with him of life and peace; and I
gave them to him for the fear wherewith he feared me, and
was afraid before my name. 6 The law of truth was in his
mouth, and iniquity was not found in his lips: he walked
with me in peace and equity, and did turn many away from
iniquity. 7 For the priest's lips should keep knowledge,
and they should seek the law at his mouth: for he is the
messenger of YHWH of hosts. (Mal 2:5-7)

So why do so many of today's ministers disregard the truth? Some seem to make it about themselves for their agenda, and not the way of truth. Righteousness of YHWH is what we are to promote as His people. To do His will, the will of the Father in Heaven is to keep HIS word and walk as He desires for us to walk. But most importantly is to do as His word says to do. Keep His Holy days, if you do not keep His Sabbath, then whose are you keeping? Any other day is not His. And what name do you call Him by His name YHWH, Yahushua or another? Think about how many times the Father name is in the Pentateuch, and the whole Old Testament, 6,500 to 7000 times. Some say it is not important. I do not think it is legalism to call the Father and Son of all creation by their true and real names, but I do think it wrong to change them and use other names. Names are not supposed to be translated, and that is a fact, ask Him what His name is and what He wants you to call Him. Because I will tell you another fact the changing of their names has caused division and deception, among those who are believers in Him and His word. Those divisions border on spiritual adultery and calling upon other mighty ones. Why do you think Yahushua said many will come to me and say master, master, and He will profess He knows them not! (Mat 7:21-23) because He is telling us all those who do not do the Father's will are not His but another's! That is why we are to become obedient to the will of the Father YHWH! And do it His way and not our own, as His scriptures say. It is of the very utmost importance for us to realize the importance of Yahweh's word. So we are not taken by the deceptions of man that has ultimately come from the deceptive spirits who are against man and YHWH. Remember the spirit of darkness is your enemy not ally. Who will stop at nothing to deceive and destroy, just like the scriptures say.

8 Be sober, be vigilant; because your adversary the devil, as a roaring lion, walketh about, seeking whom he may devour: (1Pet 5:8)

The thought may have never crossed the minds of many to search for the one who had these books written in stead of mans opinion. That is why the scriptures tell us to study, and be vigilant, so we will not fall. I once had a good friend in the faith who was a minister in a Christian ministry. He and I talked allot, one day the name of Yahushua came up in conversation and he became very angry and hard headed. Now this man was a sole winner in the Jesus name, a person who walked in faith, and was a very well known minister, who touched a lot of lives. I asked him why he was so against Yahushua as it was the saviors real name, because he was rebuking people who spoke of the savior using that real name of Yahushua, and after a slight heated discussion he said, some time ago he realized it was the saviors original name, the Hebrew name. He also said he was happy to learn this truth, and even realized a difference in the ways of Yahushua compared to the ways of what he had known. He then said, one day while in his prayer time he called on Yahushua seeking truth, and he said in his spirit he was rejected and rebuked! that devastated him badly, and he was like a evil angry advocate against Yahushua ever since. Well when I realized the importance of his reason and his speech, I seen a deception, a deception he did not see. Remember satan is a deceiver and darn good at it, he is able to falsify spiritual things and voices, false light and mimic all the ways of the Messiah. That man was falling for the lie because that is satans way, he was using that mans sense of loyalty and calling against him, by hurting his feelings. Now what does the word say: Whosoever shall call upon the name of (YHWH / Yahushua) shall be saved, you see the word cannot be broken or distorted. Yet that person believed what he heard in his heart instead of the scriptures he studied. That is a devils trick, for all to overcome, YHWH honors His word to the utmost. I also know it has happened to many people over the centuries. Some just walking into the truth get waylaid by what they hear in their spirit, and give up, or make the decision to never go into Yahushua's direction again. Hear me on this fact Yahushua the Messiah is the real name and the real way without Him there will be no hope, that is why we go through these trials. Salvation is a free gift but we have to overcome the evil works and lies against us. YHWH never told us it would be easy, but he does say to us all he that overcomes shall eat from the tree of life freely! HalleluYah!

That is a promise from His word, so stand on His truth and quit listening to satans lies. That is how Yahushua overcame satan, He quoted YHWH's words at him. This is what we must do, we must rely on the scriptures for our knowledge to overcome satans evil lies against us. I do know once a person takes that kind of a stand against Yahushua, it is not good and should not be condoned, that kind of person you must stay away from, they will poison your thinking, and besides that is the true essence of the anti-Messiah spirit or other spirits. Those are the ones that become preachers of another Messiah all because they did not follow the scriptures, instead they let man lead them and their heart that is dangerous.

9 The heart is deceitful above all things, and desperately wicked: who can know it? (Jer 17:9)

That is why many ministers are against the true name of the savior Yahushua the Messiah because of deception and not truth. Then realize the ramifications of those deceptions and all those who have followed them into the layer of the same deceptions. That is why we must be lead by the scriptures- the Spirit of the scriptures not just any man, men make mistakes. The scriptures will not teach you wrong. Usually once a deception is started in a persons mind it only continually gets worse not better, eventually it will try to keep you from truth. Then things break down, and normal things begin to be dis- regarded and eventually obsolete, new things take it's place, it is kind of like making your own way and not doing what was commanded by the Father YHWH. That is what is called teachings of men.

16 Let no man therefore judge you in meat, or in drink,
or in respect of an holyday, or of the new moon, or of the
sabbath days: 17 Which are a shadow of things to come;
but the body is of Messiah. 18 Let no man beguile you of
your reward in a voluntary humility and worshipping of
angels, intruding into those things which he hath not seen,
vainly puffed up by his fleshly mind, 19 And not holding the
Head, from which all the body by joints and bands having
nourishment ministered, and knit together, increaseth with
the increase of Elohim. 20 Wherefore if ye be dead with
Messiah from the rudiments of the world, why, as though
living in the world, are ye subject to ordinances, 21 (Touch
not; taste not; handle not; 22 Which all are to perish with
the using;) after the commandments and doctrines of men?
23 Which things have indeed a shew of wisdom in will
worship, and humility, and neglecting of the body; not in
any honour to the satisfying of the flesh.(Col 2:16-23)

That is what was meant by the teachings of men, men that maid their mind up to do what they thought to be right because of deceptions and heart felt feelings, regardless of what the scriptures say. The righteousness of man is but filthy rags to YHWH, only by His Yahushua are we accepted and able to become heirs of salvation. His Torah is as simple as keeping the Ten Commandments, yet most nations are unable to do so. Many religious groups have disregarded His Sabbath, His real name, the Sons true name because of replacement theology. Man has changed many parts of YHWH's commands for their own purpose and reasons. Almost all the man- made religions reject the clean and unclean laws because of misinterpretation and disregard for the real truth of YHWH's word. That is disobedience to His will, that is correct, (Disobedience) the scriptures are clear we are to keep the clean ordinances, for His reason, remember our bodies are His temple. He does not want His Holy Spirit in a person who does not keep his temple pure and cleansed, those things are detestable to our Savior Yahushua, those things keep us far from His presence and closer to the evil spirits. Deception is a way of the devil and many of the scriptures have been disregarded because of false gods and doctrines of demons and devils. All to keep man from the truth and salvation of YHWH. In retrospect they become tools of the evil spirit, the spirit that is against YHWH and His Son Yahushua.

That spirit of darkness uses many things to destroy others, it masquerades as a religious spirit, or anti-Messiah spirit. That same spirit tells it's followers to take another persons gift! Why? The word says do not steal, yet they think it is ok because they think they are doing gods will. That is a deception, because YHWH does not do against His word. You see if YHWH wants his minister to take any persons gift he will do it openly and not secretly, He will also do it with the person awake and aware, not drugged or subdued with any kind of hypnotic or hallucinogenic drugs, because YHWH always does His work in light to be seen by all! YHWH does not do works to be hidden, all that are His in Yahushua the Mashiyach are the tools of YHWH through Yahushua. Yahushua has His that are ministers and teachers of the good news. They usually are the targets of that other spirit, remember the other spirit is the false spirit of deception, or as the KJV puts it the anti Messiah spirit. Those who are lead by that spirit do not even know they are under a deception because that spirit has become a world wide false Messiah, teaching it's followers against Yahushua and the Father YHWH, saying the old testament no longer applies to us! Then uses the book of Galatians as a way to say the law was abolished because of faith, not so people! Other wise Yahushua died in vain and for the wrong reason, His goal was to bring us in to the spirit of favor for our completion in Him, as (sons) and no longer gentiles. So remember Paul was talking about the law of circumcision not Torah, or law in general. Because are circumcised in Messiah Yahushua, are to be obedient to the Fathers will. Paul was obedient to the will of the Father, he kept the Sabbath of YHWH and the Feasts of YHWH and was in the spirit of Yahushua the anointed one, and like wise all the apostles before him did the same. This is a reminder for us to realize who and what we serve in spirit and truth. Those who reject the son Yahushua for the man- made Greek deity are in that other spirit! Because when you reject Yahushua the son you also reject He who sent Him, and that is YHWH the creator. Now you know why Yahushua said I know you not to the many! We know Yahushua was born in Bethlehem also born Jewish, He was not American, English, Greek, or even Asian. All the scriptures were written in Hebrew or Aramaic, when they were being translated only the Greek texts were allowed to be saved, WHY? because the Romans were occupying Israel and did stay there for hundreds of years. At the time when Messiah was crucified the Romans were still doing orgies and multiple gods, like zues, the goddess estara, and many others. They had no desire or knowledge of the Messiah until after His ascension when the apostles and believers like Kepha and Phillip started to evangelize the masses and believers of false elohim. Then after Paul was killing the followers of Yahushua, he become a follower as well, a true believer in the Messiah Yahushua, now Paul also was a Hebrew by descent, and very learned in the Torah or law, the will of the Father. It does prove Yahushua can use anyone willing to speak up and witness His truth. But the real reason for Paul being converted was, the prayers of those in Yahushua Stephen was a man much like Messiah, filled with the Spirit of Yahushua.

54 When they heard these things, they were cut to the
heart, and they gnashed on him with their teeth. 55 But
he, being full of the Holy Spirit, looked up sted fastly
into heaven, and saw the glory of Elohim, and Yahushua

standing on the right hand of YHWH, [56] And said, Behold,
I see the heavens opened, and the Son of man standing on
the right hand of YHWH. [57] Then they cried out with a
loud voice, and stopped their ears, and ran upon him with
one accord, [58] And cast him out of the city, and stoned him:
and the witnesses laid down their clothes at a young man's
feet, whose name was Saul. [59] And they stoned Stephen,
calling upon Elohim, and saying, Master Yahushua, receive
my spirit. [60] And he kneeled down, and cried with a loud
voice, Master, lay not this sin to their charge. And when he
had said this, he fell asleep.(Acts 7:54-60)

When Yahushua appeared to Paul on the road to Damascus he had no idea what was happening or if he was even going to make it through his ordeal until Simon a righteous man came and told him what was going on. So you see never discount another persons purpose in Messiah Yahushua because we who are His all have a place and purpose in Him. The real reason why this has been written is for those in the belief of YHWH's word to see the true purpose in YHWH, and to help you become delivered from the lies of the false spirit that works in the hearts of man. But the main reason is because Yahushua does love us and wants us to have the best eternal home with Him. Think about the love of YHWH how long suffering and patient He has been toward us His people. The love of Yahweh our heavenly Father is the only reason I'm still alive and breathing today, otherwise I would have died as a child before my first birthday. You see YHWH has a plan and we all who believe in Him and do His will are a part of His plan. We want to be His sheep and not the goats, which only comes by His spirit in us, and us doing the will of the Father in heaven. Ok a brief overlook of what needs to be done in our lives for those who believe. The real true key is we must believe, without that, it is a waist of your time. Belief in the Father YHWH and on His son Yahushua Ha Mashiyach, our Savior.

Parents your children need to hear and believe, so read the good news to them when little children and are old enough to start understanding. Read the books of Matthew, Mark, Luke, and John to them they are stories as well as truth, they will encourage the little ones to think of Yahushua and ask questions about Him. The key is belief, they must believe Yahushua and the Father YHWH exist, that they are. Parents it is well with you to share Yahushua in love, but I caution you do not use Yahushua as a tool to punish them, that will turn them away and cause allot of problems within their minds. Now you as the parent or the adult are the one who helps them guard their precious lives against evil people and wickedness of the world that is where our daily prayer time and learning His word is a benefit to our children's futures. Men when your child is in the womb lay hands on the mommy belly and tell them of Yahushua and the Father YHWH even then. They are listening and alive hearing your words and reacting to them, and your actions.

Always remember children are a gift from YHWH to you this is how He keeps our generations going on in this life to the next. Now when your child truly believes on Yahushua the Messiah and the Father YHWH with all his or her heart you will know, I was but a child when I believed and so should your children. By the reading of the good news to them they will believe but it is when they realize it in their little hearts and minds He is, then it will be a real deal. Then after that they can become born again as scripture mentions. (John 3:3, 3:5 = Romans 10:9-13) When little children believe it is a powerful belief, and they are very precious in the eyes of Yahweh the Father. You would do good to get some blessing oil and put oil on your hand then lay that hand on them and lead them into the prayer asking Yahushua to be their Savior and guide them, speak the words according to the verses in Romans 10:9-11, then after that prayer dedicate them to Yahweh the Father and speak His protection over them to keep them from evil and terrible trials, ask the Father Yahweh in the name of Yahushua the Messiah.

Now at the age of accountability they can then be baptized in to Yahushua, remember this is when they are accountable of their own actions and mind set. They must do this when they know why and what they are doing. Now I will also say that when people have come out of the Christian walk into being a follower of Yahushua the

Messiah they all have become baptized into His real name Yahushua! (Matthew 28:18-20)

Remember Yahushua is alive and well, He is not dead nor is He a ghost so the real terminology would be Holy Spirit – (not ghost) and pronounce it like this, when they go under the water in full emersion, (By the power of the Father, and of the Son and of the Holy Spirit, I baptize you in the name of Yahushua the Messiah! Amen)

It is an order we all must confess whatever YHWH puts on their heart to confess, and call upon the Savior Yahushua the Messiah. (Rom 10:9-13) Before the full emersion baptism.

[14] Because he hath set his love upon me, therefore will I deliver him: I will set him on high, because he hath known my name. [15] He shall call upon me, and I will answer him: I will be with him in trouble; I will deliver him, and honour him. [16] With long life will I satisfy him, and show him my Salvation. (Psalm 91:14-16)

We only love Him because He first loved us, HalleluYah Praise Yah the Father in the name of Yahushua Ha Mashiyach! Amein!

One important thing to do is get a bible with the real names restored in it, for you and your family. Because it causes confusion to read the words of Yahushua when it says another name there, in His place. There are many places that have restored versions of the scriptures, you can go on line to search for the revised scriptures.

The truth is in His word, May Yahweh bless you and keep you in His light and way all your days in the name of Yahushua Ha Mashiyach, So be it!

Now think about it are you really an heir of Salvation according to YHWH's word? This is the question we all must ask our selves, we also must make sure we teach those who look to us correctly. If we take responsibility for many people we must pray for the truth daily so their blood will not be on our hands. Now remember when you go into any gathering of worship, your spirit is joining into and agreeing with the ones already joined into that group, so be careful where you worship. Ministers of the anti-Messiah spirit seek the Messianic gift of others because that gift is the true gift! HalleluYah!